THE BEST AND MOST COMPREHENSIVE IN TEST PREPARATION

9

COLLEGE BOARD ACHIEVEMENT TEST

GERMAN

Michael Busges
Instructor of German
Rutgers University, New Brunswick, New Jersey

Frederic Curry, Ph.D.
Associate Professor of German
Broward Community College, Fort Lauderdale, Florida

James V. McMahon, Ph.D.
Associate Professor of German
Emory University, Atlanta, Georgia

Linda Thomas, Ph.D.
Associate Professor of German
Randolph-Macon Woman's College, Lynchburg, Virginia

Research and Education Association
61 Ethel Road West
Piscataway, New Jersey 08854

THE COLLEGE BOARD
ACHIEVEMENT TEST IN GERMAN

Printed in the United States of America

Library of Congress Catalog Card Number 89-62085

International Standard Book Number 0-87891-688-1

CONTENTS

GERMAN ACHIEVEMENT TEST III

GERMAN ACHIEVEMENT TEST IV

GERMAN ACHIEVEMENT TEST V

GERMAN ACHIEVEMENT TEST VI

PREFACE

This book provides an accurate and complete representation of the College Board Achievement Test in German. It is composed of six complete practice tests based on the most recently administered German Achievement Tests.

Each test is one hour in length and is patterned after the actual CBAT in German. Each test covers every type of question that can be expected on the actual exam and provides an answer key with detailed and extensive explanations. Our intention is to not only provide the answers, but to also explain to the student why the answer to a particular question is more acceptable than the other possible choices, while at the same time reviewing the material most likely to be encountered on the actual exam.

By completing all six tests and studying the explanations which follow, students can discover their strengths and weaknesses and thereby become well prepared for the actual test.

ABOUT THE TEST

The College Board Achievement Test in German is offered two times during the year: December and May. Students can obtain registration forms at the school guidance or counseling office.

Although some colleges require Achievement Tests as part of the admission process, most colleges use the Achievement Test score for student placement purposes. The German test consists of 80 multiple-choice questions to be completed in one hour. The questions vary in level of difficulty and measure the gradual development of competence in the German language acquired over a period of years. Although most students who take the test have studied the language for three or four years at the high school level, some students take the test at an earlier stage in their studies.

The German Achievement Test measures your knowledge of the German language and your ability to apply that knowledge. It evaluates your reading ability in four areas necessary for mastering a language:

Vocabulary: ability to use the correct vocabulary in a particular context. Structure: ability to identify the correctness of grammatical forms. Paragraph Completion: ability to use the correct grammatical word in a particular context. Reading Comprehension: ability to recognize the main ideas in reading passages of different styles.

There are no writing, listening, or speaking sections in this exam.

The test is scored by crediting each correct answer with one point and deducting only partial credit (one-third of a point) for each wrong answer. There is no credit or deduction for questions that are omitted.

The following chart has been designed to help you find your scaled score on the CBAT German. Locate your raw score in the left hand column; the corresponding score in the right column is the actual scaled score used for the College Board Achievement Test in German.

SCORE CONVERSION TABLE

German Achievement Test

Raw Score	Scaled Score	Raw Score	Scaled Score	Raw Score	Scaled Score
80	780	45	550	10	360
79	770	44	540	9	360
78	760	43	540	8	350
77	750	42	530	7	350
76	740	41	530	6	340
75	730	40	520	5	340
74	720	39	520	4	330
73	710	38	510	3	320
72	700	37	500	2	320
71	690	36	500	1	310
70	680	35	490	0	310
69	670	34	490	-1	300
68	670	33	480	-2	300
67	660	32	480	-3	290
66	660	31	470	-4	290
65	650	30	470	-5	280
64	650	29	460	-6	280
63	640	28	460	-7	270
62	640	27	450	-8	270
61	630	26	450	-9	260
60	630	25	440	-10	260
59	620	24	440	-11	250
58	620	23	430	-12	250
57	610	22	430	-13	240
56	610	21	420	-14	230
55	600	20	410	-15	230
54	590	19	410	-16	220
53	590	18	400	-17	220
52	580	17	400	-18	210
51	580	16	390	-19	210
50	570	15	390	-20	200
49	570	14	380	-21	200
48	560	13	380	-22	200
47	560	12	370	-23	200
46	550	11	370	-24	200
				-25	200
				-26	200
				-27	200

THE COLLEGE BOARD ACHIEVEMENT TEST IN

GERMAN

TEST I

THE COLLEGE BOARD ACHIEVEMENT TEST IN

GERMAN

ANSWER SHEET

1. (A) (B) (C) (D) (E)
2. (A) (B) (C) (D) (E)
3. (A) (B) (C) (D) (E)
4. (A) (B) (C) (D) (E)
5. (A) (B) (C) (D) (E)
6. (A) (B) (C) (D) (E)
7. (A) (B) (C) (D) (E)
8. (A) (B) (C) (D) (E)
9. (A) (B) (C) (D) (E)
10. (A) (B) (C) (D) (E)
11. (A) (B) (C) (D) (E)
12. (A) (B) (C) (D) (E)
13. (A) (B) (C) (D) (E)
14. (A) (B) (C) (D) (E)
15. (A) (B) (C) (D) (E)
16. (A) (B) (C) (D) (E)
17. (A) (B) (C) (D) (E)
18. (A) (B) (C) (D) (E)
19. (A) (B) (C) (D) (E)
20. (A) (B) (C) (D) (E)
21. (A) (B) (C) (D) (E)
22. (A) (B) (C) (D) (E)
23. (A) (B) (C) (D) (E)
24. (A) (B) (C) (D) (E)
25. (A) (B) (C) (D) (E)
26. (A) (B) (C) (D) (E)
27. (A) (B) (C) (D) (E)
28. (A) (B) (C) (D) (E)
29. (A) (B) (C) (D) (E)
30. (A) (B) (C) (D) (E)
31. (A) (B) (C) (D) (E)
32. (A) (B) (C) (D) (E)
33. (A) (B) (C) (D) (E)
34. (A) (B) (C) (D) (E)
35. (A) (B) (C) (D) (E)
36. (A) (B) (C) (D) (E)
37. (A) (B) (C) (D) (E)
38. (A) (B) (C) (D) (E)
39. (A) (B) (C) (D) (E)
40. (A) (B) (C) (D) (E)
41. (A) (B) (C) (D) (E)
42. (A) (B) (C) (D) (E)
43. (A) (B) (C) (D) (E)
44. (A) (B) (C) (D) (E)
45. (A) (B) (C) (D) (E)
46. (A) (B) (C) (D) (E)
47. (A) (B) (C) (D) (E)
48. (A) (B) (C) (D) (E)
49. (A) (B) (C) (D) (E)
50. (A) (B) (C) (D) (E)
51. (A) (B) (C) (D) (E)
52. (A) (B) (C) (D) (E)
53. (A) (B) (C) (D) (E)
54. (A) (B) (C) (D) (E)
55. (A) (B) (C) (D) (E)
56. (A) (B) (C) (D) (E)
57. (A) (B) (C) (D) (E)
58. (A) (B) (C) (D) (E)
59. (A) (B) (C) (D) (E)
60. (A) (B) (C) (D) (E)
61. (A) (B) (C) (D) (E)
62. (A) (B) (C) (D) (E)
63. (A) (B) (C) (D) (E)
64. (A) (B) (C) (D) (E)
65. (A) (B) (C) (D) (E)
66. (A) (B) (C) (D) (E)
67. (A) (B) (C) (D) (E)
68. (A) (B) (C) (D) (E)
69. (A) (B) (C) (D) (E)
70. (A) (B) (C) (D) (E)
71. (A) (B) (C) (D) (E)
72. (A) (B) (C) (D) (E)
73. (A) (B) (C) (D) (E)
74. (A) (B) (C) (D) (E)
75. (A) (B) (C) (D) (E)
76. (A) (B) (C) (D) (E)
77. (A) (B) (C) (D) (E)
78. (A) (B) (C) (D) (E)
79. (A) (B) (C) (D) (E)
80. (A) (B) (C) (D) (E)

GERMAN TEST I

PART A

Time: 1 Hour
80 Questions

DIRECTIONS: Each of the sentences in this part has a blank space indicating that a word or phrase has been omitted. From the four choices select the ONE that when inserted in the sentence fits grammatically and logically with the sentence as a whole. Then blacken the corresponding space on the answer sheet.

1. Hast du ______ den Arm gebrochen?

   (A) dich

   (B) sich

   (C) dir

   (D) dein

2. Der Hund soll nur zweimal am Tage ______

   (A) essen

   (B) fressen

   (C) tafeln

   (D) schmausen

3. Der Unterricht beginnt jede(n)______ um 7 Uhr, gleich nach dem Abendessen.

   (A) Abend

   (B) Nacht

   (C) Nachmittag

   (D) Morgen

4. Max hat eine Deutschklasse jeden Mittwoch um 7 Uhr gleich nach dem Abendessen. Ihm gefällt diese(r) _____

(A) Abendunterricht

(B) Nachtklasse

(C) Nachmittagsunterricht

(D) Morgenstunde

5. Fräulein Kunz _______ jeden Morgen mit dem Bus zur Arbeit.

(A) geht

(B) reitet

(C) fährt

(D) reist

6. Die Studentin nahm ___ Band von dem Bucherregal und lies über _____ Schild und das Schwert des römischen Soldaten.

(A) das … das

(B) den … den

(C) der … dem

(D) den … das

7. Professor Schneider lehrte _______

(A) mich die deutsche Sprache

(B) mir die deutsche Sprache

(C) mich der deutschen Sprache

(D) mir der deutschen Sprache

8. Dieser Bauer wohnt außerhalb _______

(A) das Dorf

(B) des Dorfes

(C) dem Dorf

(D) dessen Dorf

9. Herr Hans Ingels war ein ausgezeichneter Pianist; er spielte einfach _______

(A) großartig

(B) farblos

(C) trotzig

(D) feige

10. Hier können wir ein Picknick abhalten, denn um uns sind nur Blumen und grünes Gras auf_______

(A) diesem Sand

(B) diesem Feld

(C) diesem Felsen

(D) dieser Wiese

11. Schnell zog sich Paul an. So hat er jetzt wieder ______

(A) Geld

(B) Kleider

(C) eine Erkältung

(D) etwas zu essen

12. Das ist der Herr, _______ gestern hier war.

(A) er

(B) wer

(C) der

(D) dessen

13. Herr Braun ist älter _______ Herr Schmidt.

(A) als

(B) dann

(C) denn

(D) wie

14. Fritz _______, wo das Hofbräuhaus steht,

(A) kann

(B) kennt

(C) weiß

(D) wird

15. denn er _______ München sehr gut.

(A) kann

(B) kennt

(C) weiß

(D) wird

16. Sie hat uns das allein machen _______

(A) ließ

(B) lassen

(C) zu lassen

(D) gelassen

17. Ich habe Paul vor einer Woche kennengelernt. Er ist ein netter _______

(A) Freund

(B) Liebling

(C) Bekannter

(D) Schatz

18. Wir klagen ihn _______ an.

(A) der Diebstahl

(B) des Diebstahls

(C) dem Diebstahl

(D) den Diebstahl

19. "Auf die Dauer wurde den Studenten das Gestammel des jungen, nervösen Professors unerträglich." Das bedeutet, _______

(A) die Studenten hören seine Vorlesung nicht.

(B) den Studenten gefällt seine Vorlesung.

(C) die Studenten mögen die Vorlesung nicht.

(D) die Studenten finden die Vorlesung sehr interessant.

20. Spricht er oft von seinem Vater? Ja, er spricht oft ______

(A) darauf

(B) davon

(C) darüber

(D) von ihm

21. ______ komme ich zu dir und bleibe______

(A) ein Tag ... der ganze Tag

(B) eines Tages ... des ganzen Tages

(C) einen Tag ... den ganzen Tag

(D) eines Tages ... den ganzen Tag

22. Auf Ihrer Liste verstehe ich diese fünf deutschen ____ nicht.

(A) Wörter

(B) Worte

(C) Worten

(D) Wort

23. Der Tisch ist sehr schön. Aber _____ ist zu groß für meine Wohnung.

(A) es

(B) er

(C) sie

(D) Sie

24. Ich kaufe _______ ein schönes Buch.

(A) mich

(B) sich

(C) mein

(D) mir

25. "Der Student hat die Bibliotheksbücher nur nach der Leihfrist zur Bibliothek zurückgebracht." Mit anderen Worten, er hat die Bücher _______

(A) gestohlen

(B) rechtzeitig zurückgebracht

(C) nie geborgt

(D) über die Leihfrist hinaus behalten

↳ to return late

26. Thomas hat alle_______ Schrauben weggeworfen.

(A) schlechte

(B) schlechter

(C) schlechtem

(D) schlechten

27. Wenn du wirklich nicht ______ , dann müßten wir dich be strafen.

(A) bezahlst

(B) bezahltest

(C) bezahlte

(D) bezahlten

28. Sammelt Hans _______ Briefmarken?

(A) alle diese

(B) alle dieser

(C) alle diesen

(D) alle diesem

29. Ist das der Wagen des _______ oder des _______?

(A) Students ... Tourists

(B) Studentes ... Touristes

(C) Studenten ... Touristen

(D) Student ... Tourist

30. Je mehr Geld wir haben, _______ besser für uns.

(A) so

(B) dann

(C) desto

(D) denn

31. Herr Braun ißt nicht im Ratskeller, _____ er ißt im Hotelrestaurant.

(A) aber

(B) sondern

(C) und

(D) wie

32. Wir haben unsere Meinung _______

(A) gewechselt

(B) verwechselt

(C) verändert

(D) geändert

33. Fritz _______ lange vor der Tür gestanden.

(A) wurde

(B) ist

(C) hat

(D) kann

34. Die Polizei _______ gestern.

(A) kam

(B) kamt

(C) kammt

(D) kamen

35. Alles, _______ er uns vorgelesen hatte, war Unsinn.

(A) das

(B) was

(C) welches

(D) wessen

36. Der Junge kaufte dem Vater gestern ein schönes Buch, und_______

(A) brachte er ihm es heute

(B) brachte er es ihm heute

(C) er brachte ihm es heute

(D) er brachte es ihm heute

37. Der Kaufmann schrieb, es _______ ein großes Problem,

(A) sei

(B) ist

(C) wird

(D) mag

38. das er aber lösen _______

(A) kann

(B) könne

(C) wird

(D) können

PART B

DIRECTIONS: Read the following passages carefully for comprehension. Each passage is followed by a number of incomplete statements or questions. Select the completion or answer that is best according to the passage and blacken the corresponding space on the answer sheet.

Mein Freund hatte ein Arbeitszimmer voll Bücher. Ich mußte ihn sofort wegen seiner Ordnung loben. Er hatte viele Bücher und hatte sie in drei Abteilungen geordnet und diese drei durch ein Schildchen gekennzeichnet. Auf dem Schild der ersten Gruppe stand: "Bücher, die ich gelesen habe." Diese Gruppe war weitaus die kleinste Gruppe. Das Schild der zweiten, genausokleinen Gruppe trug die Aufschrift: "Bücher, die ich lesen will." Die Bezeichnung der dritten, weitaus größten Gruppe lautete: "Bücher, die ich wohl nie lesen werde."

39. Man vermutet, der Freund liest Bücher

    (A) ungern

    (B) leidenschaftlich gerne

    (C) überhaupt nicht

    (D) immer wieder

40. Man vermutet weiter, sein Arbeitszimmer

    (A) ist ein schlampiges Zimmer

    (B) ist ein ordentliches Zimmer

    (C) hat wenige Bücher

    (D) hat viele Schilder

41. Der Besucher dieses Freundes hat zuerst die _______ im Arbeitszimmer gemerkt.

(A) Ordnung

(B) Abteilungen

(C) Gruppe

(D) Schilder

42. Die meisten Bücher hat der Freund _______ gelesen.

(A) schon

(B) bald

(C) nicht

(D) alle

"Ich muss Informationen über Sie, Ihre Anlageziele und Ihre Finanzmittel einholen. Es ist meine Pflicht, Ihre Aufträge zum Kauf, Verkauf oder Tausch von Wertpapieren zu führen. Nach Erhalt Ihres Auftrages habe ich die Transaktionen auf der Börse oder auf dem Markt auszuführen. Ich bin verantwortlich für die Verwahrung des Bargelds und der Wertpapiere auf Ihrem Konto bzw. In Ihrem Depot. Für die Zahlung von Geld und die Aushändigung von Wertpapieren bin ich ebenfalls verantwortlich."

43. Was bin ich von Beruf?

(A) Wissenschaftler

(B) Journalist

(C) Börsenmakler

(D) Bankier

44. Bevor dieser Herr für seine Kunden arbeiten kann, was muß er tun?

(A) Er muß die Aktien seiner Kunden kaufen, verkaufen, oder tauschen.

(B) Er muß Auskunft, unter anderem, über die Kunden sammeln.

(C) Er muß die Transaktion auf dem Markt ausführen.

(D) Er muß die Wertpapiere aushändigen.

45. Dieser Mann, während er seine beruflichen Pflichten ausführt, darf für seine Kunden Wertpapiere nicht

(A) stehlen

(B) kaufen

(C) verkaufen

(D) tauschen

46. Wo findet man meistens ein Konto?

(A) im Krankenhaus

(B) im Rathaus

(C) auf der Börse

(D) auf der Bank

Ich weiß nicht ganz genau, wo die folgende Geschichte passiert ist, aber es war in einer kleinen Stadt, die von Sandburgen und Dämmen umgeben ist. Tausende von Touristen ziehen jeden Sommer in diese Gegend.

Eines Nachts als die Mitternachtsstunde schlug, lief einer von diesen vielen Touristen eine Gasse hinunter. Alles schlief. Der Tourist blieb stehen und pochte an die Tür eines Arztes. Erschrocken sprang der Arzt aus dem Bett, ging zur Tür und öffnete sie.

Da stammelte der Tourist, es wohne eine Schwerkranke zwölf Kilometer entfernt und er bezahle gerne, wenn der Arzt sofort dahinfahre. Für zwanzig Mark würde er den Besuch machen und die ärztliche Behandlung durchführen, meinte der müde Arzt.

"Abgemacht," erwiderte der Tourist.

Wider Willen zog sich der Arzt an, holte die Arzttasche, schließ ab, und fuhr seinen Wagen aus der Garage. Der Tourist stieg ein. "Wohin?" fragte der Arzt. "Zum nächsten Dorf," gab der Tourist als Antwort.

Bald waren die beiden unterwegs zum Ziel. Sie fuhren um eine kleine Wiese und konnten in der Dunkelheit auch Kühe und einen Teil des Wattenmeers sehen. Dann fuhren sie schnell die Landstraße entlang, bis sie zum erwünschten Dorf ankamen. Sie fuhren ins Dorf hinein und als sie bald die erste Straßenkreuzung erreichten, ließ der Tourist halten, stieg aus und gab dem Arzt die zwanzig Mark.

"Aber wo ist die Kranke?" fragte der Arzt.

"Da ist keine, Herr Doktor. Der Taxifahrer in Ihrer Stadt wollte dreißig Mark für die Fahrt hierher. Da fuhr ich natürlich lieber mit Ihnen. Vielen Dank dafür! Gute Nacht! Wiedersehen!" Und der glückliche Tourist verschwand in seinem Hotel. Der Arzt aber saß noch lange mit offenem Mund hinter dem Lenkrad.

47. Wie kam der Tourist schließlich zum nächsten Dorf?

(A) Er fuhr selber dahin.

(B) Er fuhr im Taxi dahin.

(C) Er fuhr mit einer Schwerkranken dahin.

(D) Er fuhr mit einem Arzt dahin.

48. Der Erzähler dieser Geschichte weiß________, wo dieser Zwischenfall geschehen ist.

(A) ganz genau

(B) sehr genau

(C) überhaupt nicht

(D) nicht genau

49. Der Tourist ist lieber mit dem Arzt gefahren, weil der Arzt

(A) weniger Geld verlangte

(B) einen schöneren Wagen hat

(C) freundlicher als der Taxifahrer ist

(D) eine Kranke im nächsten Dorf behandeln mußte

50. Wollte der Arzt zur Schwerkranken fahren?

(A) Ja, gerne

(B) Nein, er wollte eigentlich nicht

(C) Wir haben keine Ahnung

(D) Nein, und deswegen hat er den Wunsch des Touristen abgelehnt

51. Wie kann man den Touristen am besten beschreiben?

(A) Er ist ein sehr rücksichtsvoller Mensch.

(B) Ihm ist es gleich, ob er einen anderen Menschen ausnutzt.

(C) Er hat einen Sinn für Humor.

(D) Er ist ein gerechter Mann, denn er hat ja den Arzt bezahlt.

52. Was könnte man vom Arzt sagen?

(A) Er ist ein rücksichtsloser Mensch, der seine Pflicht nicht kennt.

(B) Er ist ein dummer Mensch.

(C) Er ist ein Feigling.

(D) Er ist ein rücksichtsvoller Mensch, der seine Pflicht kennt.

53. Wie fühlt sich der Arzt sehr wahrscheinlich nach der Erklärung des Touristen beim Abschied der beiden?

(A) Der Arzt ist zufrieden.

(B) Der Arzt freut sich.

(C) Der Arzt ist erstaunt.

(D) Es ist dem Arzt alles gleichgültig.

54. Welcher Satz ist richtig?

(A) Der Tourist war krank und mußte deswegen zum nächsten Dorf.

(B) Der Tourist wollte eine kranke Bekannte besuchen.

(C) Der Tourist wollte so billig wie möglich wieder zurück zu seinem Hotel.

(D) Der Arzt wollte den Touristen wieder zu seinem Hotel zurückbringen.

PART C

DIRECTIONS: The sentences below contain blank spaces indicating omissions in the text. Below each blank are four choices. Select the choice that is grammatically correct in the context and blacken the corresponding space on the answer sheet. Be sure to read the sentences first.

Brigitte laüft ______ Bibliothekssaal, um ein Buch über Irland

55. (A) auf den
    (B) zu dem
    (C) nach dem
    (D) in den

_____ suchen, weil sie bald _____ Irland fliegt.

56. (A) so
    (B) aus
    (C) zu
    (D) an

57. (A) auf
    (B) in
    (C) nach
    (D) zu

Der Dieb_____ gestern von dem_____ Wachtmeister beobachtet.

58. (A) ist
    (B) war
    (C) wird
    (D) wurde

59. (A) Herr
    (B) Herrn
    (C) Herren
    (D) Herres

Der Dieb_____ gerade jetzt wieder von ihm beobachtet.

60. (A) ist
(B) war
(C) wird
(D) wurde

"_____ schreiben Sie?" fragte ich den Journalisten. Er

61. (A) Wer
(B) Wessen
(C) Wem
(D) Wen

antwortete, er ____ gerade über den Präsidenten, der auf der

62. (A) schrieb
(B) schrieben
(C) schreibe
(D) schreiben

Universität gewesen _____ und der zu lange geredet_____.

63. (A) ist
(B) war
(C) sei
(D) wird

64. (A) hat
(B) hatte
(C) habest
(D) habe

"_______ Kurt das letzte Mal hier war, sagte er, er wisse

65. (A) Als
(B) Wann
(C) Wenn
(D) Ob

nicht, ___ er dich wieder ____ Geburtstag besuchen kann," sagte

66. (A) als
(B) wann
(C) wenn
(D) weil

67. (A) als
(B) für
(C) zu
(D) zum

_____ mein Vater.

68. (A) mich
(B) zu mich
(C) mir
(D) zu mir

Die Mutter hat uns einen guten Kuchen_____ , und ich esse_____

69. (A) backen
(B) gebukt
(C) gebackt
(D) gebacken

70. (A) er
(B) es
(C) ihn
(D) ihm

PART D

DIRECTIONS: Read the following passages carefully for comprehension. Each passage is followed by a number of incomplete statements or questions. Select the completion or answer that is best according to the passage and blacken the corresponding space on the answer sheet.

Die Watussi meinen, dieses Tier ist der König aller Tiere, denn dieses Geschöpf ist sehr groß, stark, und stolz. Es hat keine Feinde; kein anderes Tier kann ihm ernsthaft etwas tun, und auch die schärfste Lanzenspitze macht ihm genaugenommen nicht sehr viel aus, denn seine Haut ist zu dick. Wenn es aber etwas töten, vernichten, oder zerstören will, braucht es nur daraufzutreten, ohne sich anzustrengen, weil es so viel Kraft hat. Trotz seiner Stärke aber, ist es ein gutmütiges Tier.

72. Das Tier, das hier beschrieben wird, ist

(A) der Löwe

(B) der Elefant

(C) der Gorilla

(D) die Giraffe

73. Wie wissen die Watussi, daß eine Lanze dem Tier wenige Schaden zufügen kann?

(A) Die Elefanten fressen Lanzen.

(B) Die Watussi habensich es wahrscheinlich ausgedacht.

(C) Die Watussi haben wahrscheinlich früher einmal versucht, das Tier mit Lanzen umzubringen.

(D) Es wurde ihnen von Naturwissenschaftler aus Amerika erklärt.

74. Die Watussi schätzen die _____ des Tieres am meisten.

(A) List

(B) Schüchternheit

(C) Reizbarkeit

(D) Überlegenheit

75. Die Watussi ______ dieses Tier nicht.

(A) hassen

(B) verehren

(C) mögen

(D) kennen

76. Wieso kann dieses Tier ein anderes, bloß beim Darauftreten töten?

(A) Es kann es nicht tun.

(B) Es ist so schwer und stark, daß es andere Tiere zerdrückt.

(C) Es tritt auf ein anderes und dann verprügelt es das Tier, bis es tot ist.

(D) Ein anderes Tier wird vom Anblick des großen Tieres auf der Stelle zu Tode erschrocken.

Wir kennen alle die Geschichte von dem Mann, der im Abteil eines Zuges saß und einer Dame so frech antwortete. Er rauchte eine Zigarre, also hustete die Dame. Da der Mann die Zigarre nicht weglegte, blickte die Dame streng über den Brillenrand und sagte ihm, man rauche nicht in Gegenwart einer Dame. Der Mann erwiderte ganz frech: "Wenn es Ihnen nicht gefällt, so setzen Sie sich woanders hin!" Die Frau ärgerte sich und rief: "So eine Unverschämtheit. Wären Sie mein Mann, würde ich Sie vergiften." Der Mann lächelte, rauchte weiter und sagte ihr: "Ja, und wäre ich Ihr Mann, so würde ich das Gift gerne nehmen."

77. Wer trägt hier eine Brille?

(A) Der Mann

(B) Die Dame

(C) Beide Personen

(D) Weder der Mann noch die Frau

78. Man kann annehmen, daß

(A) der Qualm der Zigarre die Dame störte

(B) der Mann der Dame gefallen hat

(C) die Zigarre der Dame gefiel

(D) die Dame auch Zigarren raucht

79. Die Antwort des Mannes, er würde das Gift nehmen, gibt zu verstehen, daß er

(A) gerne Gift nimmt

(B) sich lieber vergiften läßt, als bei dieser Frau als Ehemann zu leben

(C) der Dame das Gift geben würde

(D) gerne der Ehemann der Dame sein würde

80. Der Mann ist

(A) rücksichtsvoll

(B) gutmütig

(C) höflich

(D) ohne Anstand

THE COLLEGE BOARD ACHIEVEMENT TEST IN GERMAN

TEST I

ANSWER KEY

1.	C	21.	D	41.	A	61.	C
2.	B	22.	A	42.	C	62.	C
3.	A	23.	B	43.	C	63.	C
4.	A	24.	D	44.	B	64.	D
5.	C	25.	D	45.	A	65.	A
6.	B	26.	D	46.	D	66.	B
7.	A	27.	B	47.	D	67.	D
8.	B	28.	A	48.	D	68.	C
9.	A	29.	C	49.	A	69.	D
10.	D	30.	C	50.	B	70.	C
11.	B	31.	B	51.	B	71.	D
12.	C	32.	D	52.	D	72.	B
13.	A	33.	C	53.	C	73.	C
14.	C	34.	A	54.	C	74.	D
15.	B	35.	B	55.	D	75.	A
16.	B	36.	D	56.	C	76.	B
17.	C	37.	A	57.	C	77.	B
18.	B	38.	B	58.	D	78.	A
19.	C	39.	A	59.	B	79.	B
20.	D	40.	B	60.	C	80.	D

GERMAN TEST I

DETAILED EXPLANATIONS OF ANSWERS

1. (C)

The dative reflexive pronouns (mir, dir, sich/uns, euch, sich) are used (1) when referring to parts of the body in combination with the definite article (where English uses the possessive). This dative reflexive pronoun is used only if there is a direct object in the sentence ("Arm" in this sentence).

2. (B)

"Menschen essen, Tiere fressen." "Tafeln," reserved for people, is too fancy: "to dine, sup." "Schmausen" is rather colloquial meaning more "to feast;" a person feasts, an animal does not.

3. (A)

"Abend" is generally the time between 6 and 10 pm, and only after 10 pm can we designate the time "Nacht."

4. (A)

"Abend" is generally the time between 6 and 10 pm. After 10 pm we can designate an event with the word "Nacht." Since Max' class starts at 7 pm, it's an "evening class" in German, not a "night class" (because it begins between 6-10 pm). To be a night class, it would have to begin after 10 pm. Likewise, "I go every night at 8 pm to his house" would be rendered "jeden Abend" in German, and not "jede Nacht."

5. (C)

The generic term is "gehen." When it expresses locomotion, it indicates walking: "Er geht jeden Tag in den Park" means he walks to the park every day. But if a vehicle is involved, "fahren" must be used

unless the distance is so great that it precludes walking. If the vehicle has wheels and it is mentioned (as is here), then "fahren" must be used.
"Reiten" is used for riding animals (horses, donkeys, etc.);"reisen" is for long journeys (it means "to journey").

6. (B)
Watch nouns that have different genders and so mean different things: der Band (book volume), das Band (ribbon, tape, band, tie); der Schild (shield), das Schild (sign, door plate). The student took the book volume and read about the Roman soldier's shield (and sword). So the masculine forms are appropriate. Since both nouns are accusative singular, both "der" become "den." Likewise: der See (lake), die See (sea, ocean); der Gehalt (contents), das Gehalt (salary); der Tor (a fool), das Tor (a gate); and so on.

7. (A)
Only a select number of verbs will (must) take a double accusative. The most common of these are "lehren, nennen, fragen, schimpfen (schelten), and kosten." Thus, in the sentence above, "mich" and "Sprache" are both in the accusative case. "Es hat den Herrn drei Dollar gekostet," where "Herrn" and "Dollar" are both in the accusative, is another example of this "double accusative" concept.

8. (B)
"Außerhalb" like "innerhalb (and) oberhalb" and the more common prepositions "trotz, (an)statt, während, wegen" all require that the genitive case follow the preposition: "innerhalb des Dorfes" (within the village), "trotz des Wetters" (in spite of the weather), and so on.

9. (A)
A good synonym for "ausgezeichnet" is "großartig," especially in the expression "einfach großartig." The other adjectives/adverbs express criticism rather than praise.

10. (D)
"Feld" should be used only for ploughed, cultivated, tilled land. If it is a field of permanently green grass or a huge field of wild flowers,

weeds, etc., then "Wiese" is preferred or compounds of it (Feld- and Wiesenblumen).

11. (B)

If Paul dressed, then he is again wearing clothes. There is no indication that by getting dressed, he has or will have money, a cold, or something to eat.

12. (C)

When it's a relative pronoun, use the forms "der, die, das/die" (etc.) or "welcher, welche" (etc.), depending on gender, case, and number. "Wer" is not a relative prounoun, but rather an interrogative pronoun and so cannot be used. "Wer" is used for direct and indirect questions: "Wer ist das?" (dir. ques.); "Ich weiß nicht, wer das ist" (indir. ques.).

13. (A)

Just as the word "than" follows the comparative adjective/adverb in English (older than, slower than, more beautiful than, etc.), so also in German, the comparative adjective/adverb follows with "als": "älter als, langsamer als, schöner als," etc.

14. (C)

15. (B)

"Wissen" means to have information about something and refers to facts, situations, data, etc. Thus, it's a fact that Fritz knows where the Hofbräuhaus is. Also: "Ich weiß, zwei und zwei ist vier." I know (as a fact) two plus two is four.

"Kennen" means to be acquainted with or know a person, place or thing. Fritz knows Munich very well (a place); he knows where major attractions are, what the city has, etc. Likewise: "Ich kenne Frau Turner." "I know Mrs. Turner." I have made her acquaintance. "Ich kenne das Lied." I know that song; I've heard it before; I know the words to it.

16. (B)

As a general rule, "lassen" functions like the modals and so forms double infinitives in the perfect tenses. The auxiliary verb "haben" is always used. "Er hat das Buch liegen gelassen" sometimes occurs, but the double infinitive "liegen lassen" is preferred. This is also true of "hören" and "sehen": "Ich habe das Auto nicht kommen hören/sehen."

17. (C)
It is "Freund/in" only when it refers to very close and intimate friends on a "du" basis. Such a close friendship usually takes years to form. If it is not such a relationship, one uses "Bekannte" which means "acquaintance" as well as "friend." It always means "Bekannte" if it is on a "Sie" basis.

18. (B)
There are a few verbs that take as their object the accusative of person but the genitive of thing: "We accuse him (accusative of person) of theft (genitive of thing)": "Wir klagen ihn (acc.) des Diebstahls (gen.) an." Another example: "Wir versichern ihn (acc.) unserer Treue (gen.):" We assure him of our loyalty." A few other verbs in this category besides "anklagen" and "versichern" are "bedürfen, gedenken, sich schämen" and more.

19. (C)
If the students find the lecture to be "Gestammel" and "unerträglich," that is, they find it unbearable, then no doubt they do not like what he is doing; i.e. they do not care for his lecture.

20. (D)
A da___ compound refers only to things or ideas and not to a person. When referring back to a person, use the preposition plus pronoun, as here; von (plus) ihm.

21. (D)
To express an indefinite point in past or future time, use the genitive case. In English, it usually means "one" or "some" as here: "One day" or "Some day" ("Eines Tages"). One/some winter (eines Winters), etc. Note too: Though "Nacht" is feminine, use the masc./neuter genetive form: "One/some night" is thus "eines Nachts." To express a definitive point in time (when?) or a duration (length) of time (how long?), use the accusative case. Here: "den ganzen Tag" (acc.) because it's for how

long? For the duration of a day (duration of time).

Thus we have here: One/Some day" (Eines Tages) I'll come (to your place) and stay "for the whole day" (duration of a whole day) (den ganzen Tag).

22. (A)

"Wörter" are words used as single entities, that is, as disconnected words, such as in a list. "Worte" are words in connected discourse, that is, with a context: "Der Gast sagte ein paar freundliche Worte und setzte sich."

23. (B)

Replace nouns with pronouns that designate the same gender (and number) of the noun being replaced. Here, since "Tisch" is masculine, use the pronoun designating masculine gender nouns ("er"). When referring to a thing (e.g., a table), translate the "er" (and "sie") with "it" and not with "he" (or "she"). "Er/sie" means "he/she" only when referring to males/females.

24. (D)

The dative reflexive pronouns (mir, dir, sich/uns, euch, sich) are frequently used where more than just minimal interest is expressed (and so, called the "dative of interest"). The dative of interest is optional and occurs with verbs such as "kaufen, holen, bestellen," etc. This dative reflexive pronoun is used only if there is a direct object in the sentence ("Buch" in this sentence).

25. (D)

If the student brought the book back only after the due date, he obviously had checked them out and had returned them, although late; he did not steal them or return them on time.

26. (D)

As with the definite article (der, die, das), a modifying adjective following "alle" takes an "en" in the plural: "alle braven Kinder; alle kleinen Autos;" etc. But when demonstrative or possessive adjectives follow "alle," these dem. and poss. adjectives take the same ending that "alle" has: "alle diese; aller solcher; allen meinen;" etc. Then, in other words, there is a parallelism rather than a weak ending.

27. (B)

The general subjunctive (subjunctive II) is used for unreal conditions; i.e., situations contrary-to-fact. It can deal with the future, present, or past. To form the future and present unreal condition, use the indicative past tense form minus "t" in the third person singular (e.g., bezahlte, bezahltest, bezahlte/bezahlten, bezahltet, bezahlten) for weak verbs.

28. (A)

When demonstrative adjectives (dies-, jen-, solch-, etc.) or posessive adjectives (mein, dein, etc.) follow "alle," these adjectives will take the same ending that "alle" has: "alle diese, aller solcher, allen meinen," etc. In other words, there is a parallelism (parallel, same endings). But when modifying adjectives (not dem. or poss. adjectives) follow "alle," that modifying adjective requires weak endings (i.e., the same endings as those adjectives following the definite article ("der, die," etc.)).

29. (C)

Weak masculine nouns, also called "n-nouns," usually designate a male's station in life (profession, livelihood, activity), and they will have an "(e)n" ending in the genetive singular case, not the usual "(e)s" ending. Such nouns usually end in "t" (Student, Tourist, Polizist), in "ph" (Philosoph, Geograph), and in "nom" (Astronom). Thus, "Der Wagen des Studenten/Touristen/Philosophen/Astronomen." "Herr" and "Junge" (masculine) are included here.

30. (C)

"The more, the better; the older, the weaker" and so on; this is expressed in English with "the...the." In German this pairing is "je...desto" or "je...je" or "je...um so": "Je größer das Volumen, je kleiner der Druck" (the larger the volume, the smaller the pressure); "je billiger, desto (um so) besser fur uns" (the cheaper, (so much) the better for us).

31. (B)

Both "aber" and "sondern" convey the English "but." However, only "sondern" is correct when it meets two conditions: The first clause has some kind of negation in it, and the meaning "but on the contrary, but instead, but rather" is implied; often a contrast (difference) is inferred. Otherwise, use "aber" which means "but, however." Here, Mr. Braun is not (negative, a negation) eating in the Ratskeller but on the contrary/ but rather/but instead (sondern) he is eating in the hotel restaurant.

32. (D)

"Ändern" is best because is means "to make different" and here, to make one's mind "different" - - to change one's mind. "Wechseln" is an exchange (not a change) between two different things (e.g., money); "verändern," usually reflexive, is "to become different": "Er hat sich sehr verändert" - - he has "become different" - - he has changed a lot. "Verwechseln" means to get mixed up, confused; e.g., mix up, confuse an address and so arrive at the wrong destination: "die Adresse verwechseln".

33. (C)

Though one sees the auxiliary "sein" in the perfect tenses with this verb in the South German and in some Austrian areas, "stehen" should take a form of "haben" to form its perfect tenses.

34. (A)

"Polizei" (like "Volk") is a collective noun that takes the singular form (singular verb) in German, whereas in English "police" has a plural form (verb): "The police are coming."

35. (B)

"Was" must be used as the relative pronoun for all indefinite pronoun antecedents or when referring to an entire clause (idea). Thus "was" follows "alles, nichts, vieles, etwas," etc., and it follows an entire clause: "Sie gab mir ein schönes Buch, was mich sehr freute." "Was" refers back to the entire clause here, to the entire idea, that I was pleased that she gave me something.

36. (D)

The dative object usually precedes the accusative object, unless the accusative object is a pronoun. Here "es" (a book - ein Buch) is the neuter accusative object and so precedes "ihm" (referring to "Vater" (him)), the masculine dative (indirect) object.

In addition, it must be "er brachte" and not "brachte er" because "und" is a coordinating conjunction and does not affect word order (i.e., it takes regular, not inverted, word order).

37. (A)

38. (B)

The subjunctive is often used in indirect discourse, especially in cautious reporting (where there is some question as to the truth or accuracy of the statement by a second party) or in more formal noncommittal reporting. For indirect discourse/questions, the special subjunctive (subj. I) can be used if its form is not identical with the indicative verb forms. If it is the same, the general subjunctive (subj. II) should be used. Subj. I is formed by adding "e, est, e/en, et, en" to the verb infinitive stem; e.g., "spreche, sprechest, spreche," etc. For subj. II, add the same endings to the past tense stem (and add umlauts to "a,o,u" for strong verbs): "spräche, sprächest, spräche," etc. The special subjunctive of "sein" is "sei, seiest, sei/seien, seiet, seien."

In present time situations (present subjunctive), use only the main verb in the form(s) described above.

39. (A)

If the books that the friend probably will never read ("die ich wohl nie lesen werde") represent by far the largest group of books in the study, then we can assume he is not exactly an avid reader, though he did read some, but that was by far the smallest group ("weitaus die kleinste Gruppe").

40. (B)

The room is no doubt orderly because the visitor compliments his friend for that fact in the second sentence of the passage.

41. (A)

Of the listed items, the visitor first mentions his friend's sense of order ("sofort wegen seiner Ordnung loben").

42. (C)

Obviously, if the largest groups of books are those the friend has not yet read (the second group) and those he probably will never read (the third group), then of course most books in this study are those he has "not read" ("nicht gelesen").

43. (C)

A person who buys, sells or exchanges securities on the stock market is a stock broker and not a scientist, journalist, or banker.

44. (B)

One must first get information about a potential client before one can buy, sell or trade stocks and before one can complete buy/sell orders or deliver securities.

45. (A)

The broker can buy, sell, or trade stocks/securities for his clients, but he may not steal them for himself or for his clients.

46. (D)

One finds a money account most often in a bank, of course.

47. (D)

The cab driver asked for too much to drive the tourist. The tourist did not drive himself, and he mentioned a sick person in the next village, so the doctor drove him there.

48. (D)

The story teller states in the first sentence that he does not know exactly ("weiß nicht ganz genau") where this incident took place. He doesn't know for certain ("ganz/sehr genau"), yet he apparently has some idea.

49. (A)

The doctor charged less for his professional visit to the (imaginary) ill person than did the taxi driver. So the tourist opted to go with the doctor.

50. (B)

Most people, including the doctor, don't like to be awakened at midnight to drive a stranger somewhere. As stated, he did so "wider Willen," against his wishes, but went anyway probably because he felt a professional obligation to help a sick person.

51. (B)

It doesn't seem to bother this tourist that he (1) forced someone out of his sleep, his bed and home, at an unreasonable hour on (2) false pretenses only for (3) his selfish desire to be driven home for less than what the taxi fare is. He has "used" a person by deceiving him for his own selfish, inconsiderate gain.

52. (D)

The doctor is a caring, responsible individual who knows his duty. Otherwise, he would not have consented to drive a stranger to an unknown, rather distant place at such an unreasonable hour for a patient not known to the doctor.

53. (C)

Because he is said to be left, sitting in the car with his mouth open, "saß noch lange mit offenem mund hinterdem Lenkrad," one can only assume he is shocked and astonished at the tourist and his actions.

54. (C)

The tourist was not ill nor did he want to visit anyone who was. He simply wanted a ride back to the village where his hotel was and at the best fare possible. So he chose the doctor instead of the more expensive taxi to accomplish this.

55. (D)

Prepositions are tricky to use in any language. The English "to" in German is no exception. Generally, "to" is "an" when going toward furniture or bodies of water: "Er geht an den Tisch/See." "Zu" could also be used here. The German "in" is used when the English means "into;" i.e., use "in" when going to (into) an interior, such as into a room. Thus, "in den Bibliothekssaal, in den Wald, ins Theater," etc. "Auf" can mean "to/toward" in some expressions ("Er geht auf die Bank/ Bude/Universität"), but it generally means "on," not "to."

56. (C)

The preposition "um" requires the preposition "zu" to introduce an infinitive clause/phrase that expresses a purpose or intention. This "um" and "zu" go in pairs (um...zu) (here: "in order to look for a book about Ireland"). Likewise, "(an)statt" and "ohne" also combine with "zu" and mean "instead of" and "without": "(an)statt/ohne ein einziges Wort zu sagen" - - "instead of/without saying a single word."

57. (C)

For almost all geographical names, for all of the "3 c's" (City, Country, Continent), "nach" is used for "to." Thus, "sie fliegt nach Irland": she is flying to Ireland.

In summary (#55 and #57, above), somewhat oversimplified, but still a good guideline: an = to (furniture, water); in = into; auf = on; nach = to the 3 c's.

58. (D)
59. (B)

Weak masculine nouns, also called "n-nouns," usually designate a male's station in life (profession, livelihood, activity), and they will have an "(e)n" in all oblique cases (i.e., in all but the nominative, singular case). Thus, here the "Herr" becomes "Herrn" because "Herr Wachtmeister" is in the dative case (the name follows "von," a preposition requiring the dative). Other weak masculine nouns requiring "(e)n" in all oblique cases are "Junge, Student, Tourist, Mensch, Polizist," etc.

60. (C)

The true passive is formed by using a combination of "werden" plus the past participle (p.p.) of the main verb, and for the perfect tenses, an additional form of "sein" with a final "worden." This combination of verbs determines the English meaning and tense as follows:

Present tense:
present tense
of werden + p.p. = is/are being + p.p.
Der Brief wird geschrieben = The letter is being written

Past tense:
past tense
of werden + p.p. = was/were + p.p.
Der Brief wurde geschrieben = The letter was written

Likewise:

Present perfect tense:
present tense
of sein + p.p. + worden = has been + p.p.

Past perfect tense:
past tense
of sein + p.p. + worden = had been + p.p.

Future tense:
present tense
of werden + p.p. + werden = will be + p.p.

Future perfect tense (seldom used):
present tense
of werden + p.p. + worden + sein = will have been + p.p.

61. (C)

The indirect object (here: "To whom" are you writing?) is expressed with the dative case. This is also true of the interrogative pronoun "who" which is "wer" (nom.), "wessen" (gen.), "wem" (dat.), and "wen" (acc.).

62. (C)

The subjunctive is often used in indirect discourse, especially in cautious reporting (where there is some question as to the truth or accuracy of the statement by a second party) or in formal noncommittal reporting. For indirect discourse/questions, the special subjunctive (subj. I) can be used if its form is not identical with the indicative verb forms. If it is the same, the general subjunctive (subj. II) should be used. Subj. I is formed by adding "e,est,e/en,et,en" to the verb infinitive stem; e.g., "spreche, sprechest, spreche," etc. And here: "schreibe, schreibest, schreibe," etc. For subj. II, add the same endings to the past tense stem (and add umlauts to "a,o,u" for strong verbs): "spräche, sprächest, spräche," etc. The special subjunctive of "sein" is "sei, seiest, sei/seien, seiet, seien."

63. (C)
64. (D)

For a discussion of the subjunctive in indirect discourse, see test item number 62, above. In that item, the indirect discourse for present/future time situations was given. Here we have a past time situation. In past time situations (past subjunctive), use a "sei" form for "sein" or a subjunctive I or II form for "haben" ("er habe/hätte" etc.) plus the past participle of the main verb: "der Präsident sei gewesen" (#63) and "der Präsident habe geredet" (#64).

65. (A)

"Als" is used when the reference is to a single event or act or state in the past ("at the time when"). Here: "When Kurt was here the last time,..." Likewise: "Sie winkten, als ich abfuhr." (They waved as/ when I left.) Thus "als" will be seen with past tense forms.

66. (B)

"Wann," on the other hand, is used only as an interrogative to introduce direct or indirect questions ("at what time"): "Wann kommen Sie morgen?" Or with indirect questions (interrogative clauses): "Shirley weiß nicht, wann sie fertig ist." (Shirley doesn't know when she'll be finished. (When will Shirley be finished?)). And here: He doesn't know when (wann) he can visit you again: "..., wann er dich wieder besuchen kann."

67. (D)

Prepositions are always tricky because they can usually not be translated word for word (literally). For instance, "for" cannot always be translated with "für" or "to" with "zu." Thus, doing or receiving something for Easter, Christmas, New Year's Eve, one's birthday, etc. or being on or going for a holiday or vacation is not expressed with "für" but with just about every German preposition except "für": use "zu" for the holidays (zu Ostern/Weihnachten/Silvester; "zum" for one's birthday (zum Geburtstag); "auf " Urlaub gehen, "auf, in, im" Urlaub sein, "in" Urlaub fahren; "in" die Ferien gehen/fahren, "in" den Ferien sein, and so on.

68. (C)

It has to be "mir" because if "father tells me/said to me," then the "me" is an indirect object, and indirect objects are expressed in the dative case ("mir" is dative). The "to" in "to me" is already built into the German meaning by using the dative form. Thus, "zu mir" would be redundant "to to me" and is not correct in this sentence.

69. (D)

The forms are "backen - buk - gebacken" (it's a strong verb), though one occasionally sees "gebackt" which is probably regionalism, but not an acceptable form. "Gebukt" doesn't exist.

70. (C)

"Ich esse den Kuchen gern" becomes "Ich esse ihn gern" when using a pronoun to replace the noun (Kuchen). Stay with the gender. Since "Kuchen" is masculine, use the corresponding masculine pronoun ("er"). The "er" becomes "ihm" in the dative case and "ihn" in the accusative case. Here it is accusative because it's a direct object: "I eat it (ihn), the cake (den Kuchen)."

71. (D)

When comparing two things (here, "Kuchen" with "Torte"), use the comparative forms. (Use the superlative form when comparing more than two things.) The comparative form for "gern" (gladly) is "lieber" (more gladly) and for "gut" is "besser." These are irregular comparative forms and must be memorized.

72. (B)

Watch for certain clues: "sehr groß; Haut ... dick; braucht eß nur daraufzutreten." Of the four animals, only the elephant has a skin thick enough to withstand some spears; only it is big enough to crush something simply by standing on it. From these clues, one can infer which creature is being discussed here.

73. (C)

Obviously, the answer is not expressly stated in the passage, but using one's good judgment, a little common sense and logic, one realizes that the tribe knows this fact from personal experience when hunting animals, including the elephant, and certainly not by reading about it in a library (how may libraries are there in the plains of Africa?) or from American scientists.

74. (D)

The main impression one should derive from this passage is that the Watussi tribe feels somewhat in awe of the elephant's kind of air of superiority. The passage made no mention of whether or not elephants have cunning (choice A), shyness (choice B), or irritability.

75. (A)

Read between the lines to find that if this African tribe finds the elephant to be the king of all animals and finds it good-natured, then certainly the tribe does not hate the animal. But they certainly honor, like, and knokw about the elephant (choices B,C, and D). Read the sentence carefully and don't overlook the final "nicht." The tone of this paragraph clearly reveals that the Watussis do not despise this largest of all land animals.

76. (B)

It will crush most other animals simply by "stepping on them" because it is that big and strong: "Wenn es aber etwas töten(...) will, braucht es nur daraufzutreten, (...) weil es so viel Kraft hat."

77. (B)

The lady is wearing a pair of glasses. The clue is that she looks over the rim of her glasses to tell the man he shouldn't smoke:...blickte die Dame streng über den Brillenrand...".

78. (A)

Don't let the transposed word order of the dative case (for "gefallen") confuse you. Read it carefully. We can surely assume the smoke disturbed the lady though she never came out and said so. We can assume this since she looked at him severely and didn't hesitate to remind him of his manners about smoking in her presence.

79. (B)

He would rather poison himself than live with this woman. Though he doesn't say this, his final remark implies this and carries that message to her probably more effectively than if he had actually come out and said it.

80. (D)

We can see that the man is without much decorum, good behavior, manners (ohne Anstand). He is not caring and he doesn't sound terribly good-natured.

THE COLLEGE BOARD ACHIEVEMENT TEST IN

GERMAN

TEST II

THE COLLEGE BOARD ACHIEVEMENT TEST IN

GERMAN

ANSWER SHEET

1. (A) (B) (C) (D) (E)
2. (A) (B) (C) (D) (E)
3. (A) (B) (C) (D) (E)
4. (A) (B) (C) (D) (E)
5. (A) (B) (C) (D) (E)
6. (A) (B) (C) (D) (E)
7. (A) (B) (C) (D) (E)
8. (A) (B) (C) (D) (E)
9. (A) (B) (C) (D) (E)
10. (A) (B) (C) (D) (E)
11. (A) (B) (C) (D) (E)
12. (A) (B) (C) (D) (E)
13. (A) (B) (C) (D) (E)
14. (A) (B) (C) (D) (E)
15. (A) (B) (C) (D) (E)
16. (A) (B) (C) (D) (E)
17. (A) (B) (C) (D) (E)
18. (A) (B) (C) (D) (E)
19. (A) (B) (C) (D) (E)
20. (A) (B) (C) (D) (E)
21. (A) (B) (C) (D) (E)
22. (A) (B) (C) (D) (E)
23. (A) (B) (C) (D) (E)
24. (A) (B) (C) (D) (E)
25. (A) (B) (C) (D) (E)
26. (A) (B) (C) (D) (E)
27. (A) (B) (C) (D) (E)
28. (A) (B) (C) (D) (E)
29. (A) (B) (C) (D) (E)
30. (A) (B) (C) (D) (E)
31. (A) (B) (C) (D) (E)
32. (A) (B) (C) (D) (E)
33. (A) (B) (C) (D) (E)
34. (A) (B) (C) (D) (E)
35. (A) (B) (C) (D) (E)
36. (A) (B) (C) (D) (E)
37. (A) (B) (C) (D) (E)
38. (A) (B) (C) (D) (E)
39. (A) (B) (C) (D) (E)
40. (A) (B) (C) (D) (E)
41. (A) (B) (C) (D) (E)
42. (A) (B) (C) (D) (E)
43. (A) (B) (C) (D) (E)
44. (A) (B) (C) (D) (E)
45. (A) (B) (C) (D) (E)
46. (A) (B) (C) (D) (E)
47. (A) (B) (C) (D) (E)
48. (A) (B) (C) (D) (E)
49. (A) (B) (C) (D) (E)
50. (A) (B) (C) (D) (E)
51. (A) (B) (C) (D) (E)
52. (A) (B) (C) (D) (E)
53. (A) (B) (C) (D) (E)
54. (A) (B) (C) (D) (E)
55. (A) (B) (C) (D) (E)
56. (A) (B) (C) (D) (E)
57. (A) (B) (C) (D) (E)
58. (A) (B) (C) (D) (E)
59. (A) (B) (C) (D) (E)
60. (A) (B) (C) (D) (E)
61. (A) (B) (C) (D) (E)
62. (A) (B) (C) (D) (E)
63. (A) (B) (C) (D) (E)
64. (A) (B) (C) (D) (E)
65. (A) (B) (C) (D) (E)
66. (A) (B) (C) (D) (E)
67. (A) (B) (C) (D) (E)
68. (A) (B) (C) (D) (E)
69. (A) (B) (C) (D) (E)
70. (A) (B) (C) (D) (E)
71. (A) (B) (C) (D) (E)
72. (A) (B) (C) (D) (E)
73. (A) (B) (C) (D) (E)
74. (A) (B) (C) (D) (E)
75. (A) (B) (C) (D) (E)
76. (A) (B) (C) (D) (E)
77. (A) (B) (C) (D) (E)
78. (A) (B) (C) (D) (E)
79. (A) (B) (C) (D) (E)
80. (A) (B) (C) (D) (E)

GERMAN TEST II

PART A

Time: 1 Hour
80 Questions

DIRECTIONS: Each of the sentences in this part has a blank space indicating that a word or phrase has been omitted. From the four choices select the ONE that when inserted in the sentence fits grammatically and logically with the sentence as a whole. Then blacken the corresponding space on the answer sheet.

1. Er hat es immer ________ .

   (A) schnell

   (B) rasch

   (C) eilig

   (D) geschwind

2. Ich bin ________ nach Deutschland gefahren.

   (A) in 1987

   (B) im Jahre 1987

   (C) am Jahre 1987

   (D) im Jahr 1987

3. Brahms ________ am 7. Mai 1833 geboren.

   (A) wird

   (B) werde

   (C) wurde

   (D) ist

4. __________ kommt er zu mir.

(A) Hin und her

(B) Auf und ab

(C) Ab und zu

(D) Hier und dort

5. __________bringt Briefe.

(A) Der Postmann

(B) Der Briefbringer

(C) Der Postträger

(D) Der Briefträger

6. Wo __________ du die Schule?

(A) gehst

(B) besuchst

(C) lernst

(D) unterrichtest

7. Ich denke nicht ________.

(A) daran

(B) an dem

(C) woran

(D) voran

8. Er hat __________, hier zu bleiben.

(A) die Absicht

(B) die Aussicht

(C) die Sicht

(D) die Aufsicht

9. Das ist ________alles völlig egal.

(A) mich

(B) mir

(C) meinetwegen

(D) ihn

10. _________ kommst du _____ er.

(A) Entweder...noch

(B) Entweder...oder

(C) weder...oder

(D) wieder...noch

11. Er _________ die Frage.

(A) verantwortet

(B) antwortet

(C) beantwortet auf

(D) beantwortet

12. Er ist ______ alt ______ ich.

(A) als…als

(B) so…als

(C) so…wie

(D) als…wie

13. Ich habe ________ _____ dem Zahnarzt.

(A) Angst vor

(B) Angst für

(C) Angst an

(D) Ängste vor

14. ________________ Briefe hast du denn von ihm bekommen?

(A) Was vor

(B) Was Für

(C) Was für einen

(D) Welche für

15. Hast du das Gedicht ___________ ___________?

(A) inwendig gelernt

(B) auswendig gelesen

(C) auswendig gelernt

(D) auswendig gelehrt

16. Ist das wirklich ____________________?

(A) der Mühe wert

(B) die Mühe wert

(C) des Mühes wert

(D) wert der Mühe

17. Ich interessiere mich ________ die Musik von Mozart.

(A) in

(B) für

(C) auf

(D) an

18. Helfen Sie ______ doch!

(A) ihn

(B) sie

(C) ihm

(D) es

19. Er hat sich hoffnungslos in _______________.

(A) mich beliebt

(B) mich verliebt

(C) mir verliebt

(D) mich geliebt

20. Das ist der Mann, ______ ich gestern sah.

(A) der

(B) die

(C) dem

(D) den

21. Er stellte die Flasche auf ________ Tisch.

(A) dem

(B) der

(C) die

(D) den

22. Ich habe ______________________gearbeitet.

(A) der ganze Tag

(B) den ganzen Tag

(C) dem ganzen Tag

(D) des ganzen Tages

23. Er weiß nicht, __________ ich bin.

(A) wer

(B) der

(C) wen

(D) wem

24. Wann kommt er gewöhnlich _______________?

(A) zu Hause

(B) nach Hause

(C) in dem Haus

(D) nach dem Haus

25. Leider habe ich ________ Geld.

(A) nicht

(B) keins

(C) kein

(D) nein

26. Gefällt ______ sein Haus?

(A) dich

(B) dir

(C) sie

(D) ihn

27. "________ zuletzt lacht, lacht am besten."

(A) Wer

(B) Wen

(C) Wem

(D) Wo

28. Wann kommt er ________?

(A) vor

(B) an

(C) in

(D) zu

29. ____ das ____ verstehen, mußt du das Buch lesen.

(A) In...Ordnung

(B) Um...zu

(C) Um...nach

(D) In...zu

30. Wir haben etwas ___________ zu berichten.

(A) Wichtiges

(B) Wichtigen

(C) Wichtig

(D) Wichtiger

31. Ein _______________war bei uns zu Besuch.

(A) Deutsch

(B) Deutsche

(C) Deutscher

(D) Deutschen

32. _______________ kam er unerwartet.

(A) Ein Tag

(B) Eines Tages

(C) Einen Tag

(D) Einem Tag

33. Ich weiß nicht __________ er meint.

(A) was

(B) welchem

(C) wer

(D) wem

34. Ich erinnere __________ noch an die Zeit in Wien.

(A) sich

(B) selbst

(C) mich

(D) mir

35. Bist du verrückt? __________ doch langsam!

(A) Fähr

(B) Fährst

(C) Fahrt

(D) Fahre

36. Es ______________ viele Leute, die gern Fußball spielen.

(A) gibt

(B) geben

(C) sind

(D) ist

37. ________ ich dort wohnte, war ich jung.

(A) Wenn

(B) Als

(C) Wann

(D) Obwohl

38. Wohnt er ____________________ in Köln?

(A) immer nicht

(B) immer noch

(C) immer wieder

(D) immer mehr

PART B

DIRECTIONS: Read the following passages carefully for comprehension. Each passage is followed by a number of incomplete statements or questions. Select the completion or answer that is best according to the passage and blacken the corresponding space on the answer sheet.

Im Jahre 1284 erschien ein merkwürdiger Mann in Hameln. Er trug einen vielfarbigen, bunten Rock and behauptete Rattenfänger zu sein. Er sagte, er könnte gegen ein gewisses Geld die Stadt von allen Mäusen und Ratten befreien. Die Bürger erklärten sich bereit, diesen Lohn zu bezahlen. Der Rattenfänger zog sein Pfeifchen heraus und spielte. Ratten und Mäuse krochen aus allen Häusern hervor and sammelten sich um ihn herum. Als er meinte, daß alle da waren, ging er aus der Stadt hinaus. Der genze Haufen folgte ihm, stürzte ins Wasser und ertrank. Als die Bürger sich von ihrer Plage befreit sahen, wollten sie nicht mehr den Lohn bezahlen. Der Mann ging verbittert weg. Kurz danach kehrte er zurück. Diesmal war er als Jäger gekleidet und trug einen roten, wunderlichen Hut. Während alle Bürger in der Kirche versammelt waren, ließ er seine Pfeife wieder in den Gassen ertönen. Jetzt kamen nicht Ratten und Mäuse, sondern Kinder, vom vierten Jahr an, gelaufen. Diese führte er hinaus und verschwand. Nur zwei Kinder wurden gerettet. Das eine war blind und konnte den Ort nicht zeigen und das andere war stumm und konnte nicht erzählen. Es war ganze 1340 Kinder verloren. (Nach Bruder Grimm "Deutsche Sagen")

Die Sage ist eine der bekanntesten Sagen in aller Welt. Sie wurde in ca. 30 Sprachen übersetzt und gehört in vielen Ländern zum Standardprogramm im Schulunterricht. Ihre genaue Kläung ist bis heute nicht möglich gewesen. Sie besteht jedoch aus einer Verbindung von verschiedenen Geschichten, die zur Zeit der Rattenplagen in Europa entstanden sind. Es ish wahrscheinlich, daß es zu der Zeit Rattenfänger gab, aber sie haben bestimmt realistischera Methoden verwendet als der sagenhafte Rattenfänger von Hamelin.

39. Der Mann behauptete,

(A) er könnte dia Stadt umsonst von Ratten befreien.

(B) er könnte Ratten und Mäuse von der Stadt entfernen.

Ratten befreien.

(D) er könnte gegen ein gewisses Geld die Kinder aus der Stadt führen.

40. Was war des Resultat seines Spielens?

(A) Die Bürger wollten das Geld nicht bezahlen.

(B) Die Ratten folgten ihm in die nächste Stadt.

(C) Die Ratten sind im Fluß umgekommen.

(D) Ein Haufen Bürger stürzte ins Wasser und ertrank.

41. Was war das Resultat seines Erfolgs?

(A) Er ging enttäuscht und unglücklich weg.

(B) Die Leute wollten den Lohn nicht bezahlen, aber er bekam ihn trotzdem.

(C) Er verkleidete sich als Jäger und erschoß die Bürger der Stadt.

(D) Er bekam endlich sein Geld.

42. Diese Sage

(A) ist in aller Welt weniger bekannt, als andere Sagen.

(B) wird oft in Schulen gelesen.

(C) ist heute völlig geklart worden.

(D) hat nichts mit dem Leben im 13. Jehrhundert zu tun.

Wegen des engen Zusammenlebens in einer Großstadt kann es oft zu Streit swischen Nachbarn kommen. Die Chancen für solche Streiterein steigen, wenn Tiere auf der Bildfläche erscheinen. Das war der Fall in einem ländlichen Stadtteil von München, wo ein Jurist einen Nachbarn mit einem Hahn namens "Fredi" hatte. Der entnervte Jurist behauptete Fredis Krähen sei genauso störend wie der Lärm von Baumaschinen. Da Baumaschinen zwischen 22 und 7 Uhr nicht benutzt werden dürfen, sollte Fredi auch nicht während dieser Zeit krähen dürfen. Vor dem Landgericht in München wurde Fredi aber dazu verurteilt, täglich von 20 bis 8 Uhr in seinem schalldichten, (sound proof) Stall eingesperrt zu werden. Das war also länger als die Ruhezeit für Baumaschinen. An Sonn-und Feiertagen durfte er auch nicht zur Mittagszeit frei herumlaufen. Fredis Besitzer war nicht damit zufrieden und es gab einen zweiten Prozeß. Diesmal kam Fredi besser davon weg. Als Resultat dieses Prozeßes mußte Fredi nur noch zur üblichen Ruhezeit zwischen 22 und 7 Uhr den Schnabel halten.

43. In einer Großstadt gibt es oft Schwierigkeiten zwischen Nachbarn, weil

(A) man wenig Platz hat.

(B) man gern streitet.

(C) man die Nachbarn nicht mag.

(D) Tiere mit einander streiten.

44. Warum beklagte sich Fredis Nachbar?

(A) Weil Fredi seine Baumaschine kaputtmachte.

(B) Weil Fredi viel Lärm machte.

(C) Weil Fredi entnervt war.

(D) Weil Fredi zwischen 22 und 7 Uhr die Baumaschine benutzte.

45. Warum war Fredis Strafe ungerecht?

(A) Weil Fredis Kräden doch nicht so störend war, wie die Baumaschine.

(B) Weil Fredi in einem Stall eingesperrt werden mußte.

(C) Weil Fredi länger sein mußte, als die Baumaschine.

(D) Weil Fredi keine Baumaschine war, sondern ein Hahn.

46. Warum war der zweite Prozeß günstiger für Fredi?

(A) Jetzt mußten die Baumaschine zwischen 20 und 8 Uhr ruhig sein.

(B) Jetzt durfte sein Besitzer frei herumlaufen.

(C) Jetzt durfte Fredi weggehen.

(D) Jetzt durfte Fredi längere Zeit krähen.

Wie wird man Rock Star in der Deutschen Demokratischen Republik? Die Antwort auf diese Frage findet man in der Lebensgeschichte von Tamara Danz, der bekanntesten Sängerin der DDR. Tamara Danz gilt als "deutsche Tina Turner." Nach ersten musikalischen Versuchen auf Partys und kleinen Veranstaltungen, schien sie zuerst den normalen Weg einschlagen zu wollen. Sie immatikulierte sich an der Humbolt-Universität für das Fach Germanistik. Nebenbei trat sie als Sängerin einer Rockgruppe auf. In ihrer Studienzeit lernte sie andere Sänger in Ostberlin kennen und beschloß, ihr bisheriges studentisches Leben aufzugeben. Stattdessen wollte sie an der Berliner Hochschule für Musik weiterstudieren, aber diese Hoffnung erfüllte sich nicht. Später behauptete sie, das wäre das Beste, was ihr hätte passieren können, weil die meisten Hochschulabsolventen in der rockmusik keinen Erfolg haben. Aber in der DDR muß man einen Berufsausweis für Musiker haben. Um in den Besitz dieses Ausweises zu gelangen, besuchte Tamara Danz eine kleine Musikschule in Berlin, wo Klavier und Gesang im Vordergrund standen. Über ihre Ausbildung behauptet Tamara Danz, sie habe sich selbst alles beibringen müssen, was sie kann, aber die Ausbildung schade nichts, man werde schließlich nicht blöder devon. Im Jahre 1978 entstand ihre Band "Silly." Jetzt ist diese Gruppe "Meilenstein" in der DDR-Rockgeschichte erklärt. Sie plant Tourneen durch die Schweiz und Westdeutschland und träumt vom Auftritt in London, fürchtet aber, daß die Engländer sich wenig für deutschsprachige Texte interessieren.

47. Dieser Aufsafz stellt die Frage wie

(A) man Rockstar in Westdeutschland wird.

(B) man überhaupt Rockstar wird.

(C) man eine deutsche Tina Turner wird.

(D) man Rockstar im anderen Teil Deutschlands wird.

48. Tamara Danz

(A) wollte an der Berliner Hochschule für Musik studieren.

(B) wollte vom Anfang an Germanistik studieren.

(C) wollte nur nebenbei als Sängerin auftreten.

(D) wollte ihr bisheriges studentischen Leben weiterführen.

49. Was hält sie davon, daß ihr Auftrag für die Berliner Hochschule für Musik abgelehnt wurde?

(A) Sie ist immer noch sehr enttäuscht.

(B) Sie freut sich.

(C) Sie hofft immer noch, dort angenommen zu werden.

(D) Sie glaubt, die Hoffnung wird sich erfüllen.

50. Warum besuchte sie eine kleine Musikschule in Berlin?

(A) Weil man doch Klavier lernen muß.

(B) Weil sie einen Berufsausweis brauchte.

(C) Weil Klavier und Gesang bei ihr im Vordergrund stehen.

(D) Weil die kleine Schule besser ist als die größere.

51. Über die Ausbildung sagt Tamara Danz:

(A) Die Ausbildung ist blöd.

(B) Man wird schließlich dümmer davon.

(C) Man kann doch etwas davon lernen.

(D) Sie mußte alles selbst lernen.

52. Die vorletzte LP der Band "Silly"

(A) wird für wichtig gehalten.

(B) wird für die Rockgeschichte für unbedeutend gehalten.

(C) wird gar nicht von den Kritikern beachtet.

(D) machte die Gruppe Nr. 1 in der DDR.

53. Was hält Tamara Danz von einem Auftritt in London?

(A) Sie fürchtet, den Engländern würde ihre Musik nicht gefallen.

(B) Sie fürchtet, die Engländer würden die deutschen Texte nicht interessant finden.

(C) Sie denkt nicht daran.

(D) Sie will nur Westdeutschland und die Schweiz besuchen.

PART C

DIRECTIONS: The sentences below contain blank spaces indicating omissions in the text. Below each blank are four choices. Select the choice that is grammatically correct in the context and blacken the corresponding space on the answer sheet. Be sure to read the sentences first.

In Berlin __________ der __________ Mann __________

54. (A) hat
    (B) hatte
    (C) wurde
    (D) ist

55. (A) junger
    (B) jung
    (C) jungen
    (D) junge

56. (A) jeden Abend
    (B) jedar Abend
    (C) jedes Abend
    (D) jede Abend

____________________ Theater gegangen.

57. (A) ins
    (B) in
    (C) in der
    (D) in den

_______________er Zeit und Geld gehabt, __________er länger

58. (A) Hat
    (B) Hatte
    (C) Habe
    (D) Hätte

59. (A) wäre
    (B) war
    (C) hätte
    (D) hatte

In Deutschland geblieben, ______________________________.

60. (A) und einen Roman schreiben
(B) um einen Roman zu schreiben
(C) um einen Roman schreiben
(D) um zu schreiben einen Roman

Helga ist eine ________________ Dame, ________________ in der

61. (A) altere
(B) ältere
(C) alteren
(D) alter

62. (A) die
(B) wer
(C) welcher
(D) wo

Nachbarschaft ________________________.

63. (A) arbeite
(B) gearbeitet ist
(C) arbeitete
(D) gearbeitet war

________________________ Mutter wohnte bei ____________________.

64. (A) Ihre
(B) Seiner
(C) Ihrer
(D) Sein

65. (A) sie
(B) dich
(C) ihr
(D) mich

______________Frühling gibt es immer noch viele ______Tage.

66. (A) Im
(B) In der
(C) Zu
(D) In

67. (A) kalten
(B) kalte
(C) kalt
(D) kalter

Er ______________ neben __________, weil wir unsere Reise

68. (A) standete
(B) stande
(C) stand
(D) stehte

69. (A) mich
(B) mir
(C) mein
(D) meiner

________________________________.

70. (A) zu besprechen wollten
(B) besprechen wollten
(C) besprechen gewollt
(D) besprechen wollt

PART D

DIRECTIONS: Read the following passages carefully for comprehension. Each passage is followed by a number of incomplete statements or questions. Select the completion or answer that is best according to the passage and blacken the corresponding space on the answer sheet.

Der bekannte Dichter Bertolt Brecht war eine Art Lebanskünstler, der es verstand, sich in schwierigen Lagen durchzuschlagen, ob in Nazi-Deutschland, in Amerika, oder in der späteren DDR. Daß diese Überlebens-Fähigkeit sich ziemlich früh merken ließ, sieht man in einer Geschichte, die von einem Schulkameraden aus ihrer gemeinsamen Schulzeit erzählt wurde. Eines Tages bekamen die Schüler schriftliche Arbeiten zurück, die vom Klassenlehrer korrigiert worden waren. Bei Brecht gab es viele Fehler, die nicht zu übersehen waren, wegen des roten Stiftes, den der Lehrer reichlich benutzt hatte. Da er für diese Arbeit eine schlechte Note bekam, war Brecht unzufrieden. Nach kurzer Überlegung nahm er selber einen roten Stift und umkreiste einige Antworte, die richtig waren. Dann nahm er die Arbeit wieder zum Lehrer, zeigte auf die neuen "Fehler" und fragte, wieso die Antworten falsch seien. Der Lehrer sah sie sorgfältig an und gab dann zu, er habe sich offenbar geirrt und einiga richtige Antworte aus Versehen für falsch gehalten. Es blieb ihm keine Wahl. Er mußte die von Brecht umkreisten Punkte zu der ersten, schlechten Note rechnen, mit dem Resultat, daß Brecht am Ende eine befriedigende Note hatte.

71. Bertolt Brecht gilt als Lebenskünstler, weil

(A) er viele Gedichte schrieb.

(B) er bekannt war.

(C) er andere geschlagen hat.

(D) er sich in schwierigen Zeiten retten konnte.

72. Da Brecht mit seiner Note unzufrieden war,

(A) hat er seine Arbeit weggeworfen.

(B) umkreiste er einige richtige Antworten, als ob sie falsch wären.

(C) zeigte er den Lehrer an.

(D) umkreiste er einige falsche Antworten, als ob sie richtig wären.

73. Was machte der Lehrer, als Brecht ihm die Arbeit wieder zeigte?

(A) Er behauptete, Brecht habe sich geirrt.

(B) Er sagte, Brecht habe keine Wahl. Er müßte die Note akzeptieren.

(C) Er sagte, Brechts Note wäre schon befriedigend.

(D) Er dachte, er hatte sich geirrt und gab Brecht eine bessere Note.

74. Diese Geschichte zeigt, daß

(A) Brecht schlau, aber nicht immer ehrlich, war.

(B) Brecht ein braver, gehorsamer Schuler war.

(C) Brecht Angst vor seinem Lehrer hatte.

(D) Brecht immer ohne Weiteres befriedigende Noten bekam.

Ein Deutscher, der nie in Amerika war und wenig Englisch konnte, hatte große Lust, San Francisco kennenzulernen. Obwohl er Angst vorm Fliegen hatte, nahm er sich zusammen und kaufte ein Flugticket nach Kalifornien. Der Flug war lang, aber angenehm und alles lief planmäßig. Als das Flugzeug in Amerika landete,verstand er nicht, was angesagt wurde, aber er freute sich, endlich aus dem Fluzeug aussteigen und die Beine ausstrecken zu können. Drei Tage lang besichtigte er die Stadt, aber er wunderte sich, daß sie so klein war. Endlich kam er zum Schluß, daß er in einem Vorort und nicht im Stadtzentrum von San Francisco war. Also stieg er in ein Taxi ein und sagte dem Taxifahrer, er möchte ins Stadtzentrum fahren. Der Taxifahrer war verblüfft, weil sie schon da waren. Er wollte jedoch den deutschen Touristen nicht beleidigen und fragte ihn so höflich wie möglich, in welches Stadtzentrum er denn fahren möchte. Der Deutsche sagte etwas empört, daß er selbstverständlich ins Stadtzentrum von San Francisco fahren wollte. Der Taxifahrer sah ihn fassungslos an und erklärte ihm, das sei mindestens 3000 Meilen von dieser Stadt entfernt. Jetzt war der Deutsche fassungslos, aber es gelang ihm doch den Taxifahrer zu fragen, in welcher Stadt er nun sei. Es stellt sich heraus, daß sein Flugzeug eine Zwischenlandung in Bangor, Maine hatte und er war ungefähr vier Stunden und 3000 Meilen zu früh ausgestiegen. Nachdem es dem Taxifahrer klar wurde, was passiert war, fand er die Geschichte ganz lustig, und sie kam in die Bangorer Zeitung. Daraufhin wurde der Deutsche vom Bürgermeister und verschiedenen Bürgern der Stadt-Bangor eingeladen. Er blieb noch zwei Wochen dort und ist wegen der Gastfreundlichkeit in Bangor nie weiter nach San Francisco gefahren. Am Ende der Zeit ist er ganz vergnügt wieder ins Flugzeug eingestiegen, um nach Deutschland zurückzufliegen. Beim Abschied teilte er den Bürgern von Bangor mit, er hätte vor, nächstes Jahr wieder seinen Urlaub bei ihnen zu verbringen.

75. Warum ist der Deutsche falsch ausgestiegen?

(A) Er verstand nicht genug Englisch.

(B) Er wollte die Stadt Bangor besichtigen.

(C) Der Flug war ihm zu lang.

(D) Er wollte die Beine ausstrecken.

76. Warum stieg er in ein Taxi ein?

(A) Er war müde.

(B) Er wollte ins Stadtzentrum fahren.

(C) Er wollte einen Vorort von San Francisco sehen.

(D) Er wollte 3000 Meilen mit dem Taxi fahren.

77. Der Taxifahrer war verblüfft, weil

(A) sie schon in San Francisco waren.

(B) der Deutsche ihn beleidigte.

(C) er den Deutschen nicht beleidigen wollte.

(D) sie bereits im Stadtzentrum waren.

78. Der Deutsche war fassungslos, weil

(A) der Taxifahrer nicht fahren wollte

(B) er nicht gewußt hatte, daß das Flugzeug eine Zwischenlandung hatte.

(C) er San Francisco doch nicht besuchen wollte.

(D) der Taxifahrer 3000 Meilen in 4 Stunden fahren wollte.

79. Der Deutsche

(A) war überall zu Gast.

(B) fand die Gastfreundlichkeit in Bangor unausstehlich.

(C) ist sofort weiter nach San Francisco gefahren.

(D) wollte nächstes Jahr unbedingt nach San Francisco fahren.

80. Die Geschichte zeigt, was passieren kann, wenn

(A) man nach San Francisco fährt.

(B) man die Sprache nicht beherrscht.

(C) man aus einem Flugzeug aussteigt.

(D) man einen Taxifahrer etwas fragt.

THE COLLEGE BOARD ACHIEVEMENT TEST IN GERMAN

TEST II

ANSWER KEY

1.	C	21.	D	41.	A	61.	B
2.	B	22.	B	42.	B	62.	A
3.	C	23.	A	43.	A	63.	C
4.	C	24.	B	44.	B	64.	A
5.	D	25.	C	45.	C	65.	C
6.	B	26.	B	46.	D	66.	A
7.	A	27.	A	47.	D	67.	B
8.	A	28.	B	48.	A	68.	C
9.	B	29.	B	49.	B	69.	B
10.	B	30.	A	50.	B	70.	B
11.	D	31.	C	51.	D	71.	D
12.	C	32.	B	52.	A	72.	B
13.	A	33.	A	53.	B	73.	D
14.	B	34.	C	54.	D	74.	A
15.	C	35.	D	55.	D	75.	A
16.	A	36.	A	56.	A	76.	B
17.	B	37.	B	57.	A	77.	D
18.	C	38.	B	58.	D	78.	B
19.	B	39.	B	59.	A	79.	A
20.	D	40.	C	60.	B	80.	B

GERMAN TEST II

DETAILED EXPLANATIONS OF ANSWERS

1. (C)

All of the choices have to do with being fast. However, only the word "eilig" fits here. The words "es" and "hat" reveail it to be part of the idiom "es eilig haben." The English equivalent is "to be in a hurry." "Schnell," "rasch," and "geschwind" all mean "fast."

Examples: Er läuft schnell. (He runs fast).
Er entschließt sich oft zu rasch. (He often decides hastily).
Das geht nicht so geschwind. (That doesn't go so fast).

2. (B)

There are two possibilities in German for expressing the English equivalent of "in the year____." One can either say "im Jahre_____" or simply state the year without a preposition. for example, the above sentence could also read: "Ich bin 1987 nach Deutschland gefahren." Choice (A) is one of the most common mistakes made by English speaking students of German, because it is closest to English. Remember, either the whole phrase or nothing. The preposition "am" in (C) is used before days of the week (am Montag, am Dienstag etc.), or for dates in which the day is also given: Am 1. Juli 1987. The preposition "zu," like all prepositions, has many uses, but in time expressions it appears only in the expression "zu Weihanachten," which means "at Christmas."

3. (C)

To state the birth date of a deceased person, the imperfect of the verb "werden" is used. For a living person, the present of "sein" is used: "Ich bin 1959 geboren." Since Brahms is no longer living, choice D is incorrect. (A) is incorrect because it is the present tense of the verb "werden." (B) is the first person singular present tense of the verb "werden." It is incorrect because it is the wrong tense and also because it would have to be third person singular to agree with the subject "Brahms."

4. (C)

"Ab and zu" means "now and then" and fits the context of the sentence. All other choices listed have to do with location. Choice (A), "hin und her," does not fit because it means "back and forth." Choice (B), "auf und ab," means "up and down." Choice (D), "hier and dort," is the equivalent of "here and there" in English.

5. (D)

Choice (A) is a literal translation of "mailman" and does not exist. Choice (B) is also an invention and literally means "letter bringer." Choice (C) is a combination of fact and fantasy. The words "Post" and "Träger" exist, but not in this combination. The correct answer, "Briefträger" means literally "letter carrier." "Träger" is a noun derived from the verb "tragen," "to carry."

6. (B)

"Eine Schule besuchen" is an idiom meaning "to attend school." The other choices all have to do with school, but would have to be used with a preposition:

- (A) Gehst du heute in die Schule? (Are you going to school today?)
- (C) Was lernst du in der Schule? (What are you learning at school?)
- (D) Unterrichten Sie in dieser Schule? (Do you teach in this school?

7. (A)

"Daran" is a "da(r)-construction." It replaces a preposition + a pronoun referring to a thing. "Ich denke nicht daran" means "I am not thinking about it." If the sentence were "I am not thinking about him," it would not be possible to express the prepositon + pronoun with the" da(r) - construction": "Ich denke nicht an ihn." Choice (B) is not possible, because the expression "denke an" is always followed by the accusative and "dem" is dative. Choice (C) is a "wo(r) - construction" and is used to replace a preposition + "was." For example: "Woran denkst du?" (What are you thinking about?) Choice (D) simply means "ahead" and does not fit. An example of its use would be" "Er geht voran." (He's going ahead).

8. (A)

"Die Absicht haben" means "to have the intention." Choices (B) and (C) mean "view" and do not fit the context. Examples of their use are:

Von dem Fenster im Hotel hatte er eine schöne Aussicht. (From the hotel window he had a beautiful view.)

Bei diesem Wetter ist die Sicht gut. (The view/visability is good in this weather.)

Choice (D) has to do with watching over and supervising:

Sie hatten die Aufsicht über die Kinder. (They were in charge of the children.)

9. (B)

The idiom "Das ist mir egal" means "That's all the same to me" or "I don't care." The person who doesn't care is always in the dative case. For example, "He doesn't care" would be: "Das ist ihm egal." Since none of the other forms given are dative, they are incorrect. Choice (A) is the accusative form of the first person singular pronoun.Choice (C) "meinetwegen" means "as far as I am concerned" or "for my sake and on my account." Examples:

Meinetwegen brauchst du das nicht zu tun. (You don't have to do that on my account.)

Darf ich mitkommen? Meinetwegen. (May I come along? As far as I'm concerned.)

10. (B)

The English equivalent of "entweder...oder" is "either...or." The sentence reads: "Either you come, or he [comes]." The combinations in (A), (C), and (D) do not exist. The other legitimate form is "weder...noch." It means "neither...nor." Example:

Weder mir noch ihm gehört das Buch.
(The book belongs to neither me nor him.)

11. (D)

There are two ways to express "to answer a question" in German. One is "beantworten" + the accusative case and the other is "antworten" + "auf" + the accusative case. Choice (B) is incorrect, because "antworten" would have to be followed by "auf." Choice (A) is from the verb "verantworten." It means "to answer for" or "to account for." Choice (C) is wrong, because the preposition "auf" is used with "beantworten."

12. (C)

In comparing two things that are equal, the combination "so...wie" is used. The English equivalent is "as...as." Choice (A) is a direct translation of the English equivalent and is incorrect. The combinations in (B) and (C) do not exist.

13. (A)

In order to answer this correctly, you must know the German idiom "Angst haben vor," which means "to be afraid of." The preposition is always "vor." Therefore choices (B) and (C) are incorrect. The word for "fear" in Choice (D) is plural. It always remains singular in this expression.

14. (B)

"Was für" means "what kind of." The sentences reads "What kind of letters did you receive from him?" The combination in choices (A) and (D) do not exist. Choice (C) is possible. It means "what kind of a." Since "einen" is masculine accusative, it would have to be used in a sentence in which it is followed by a masculine direct object. For example:

Was für einen Koffer hattest du?

(What kind of a suitcase did you have?)

15. (C)

In order to answer correctly, you need to know the expression "etwas auswendig lernen." The English equivalent is "to learn something by heart." The other combinations are not possible. The word "inwendig" in choice (A) means "internal." In choice (B) "gelesen" is the past participle of the verb "lesen," "to read." In choice (D), "gelehrt" is the past participle of the verb "lehren," which means "to teach." None of these can be used with "auswendig."

16. (A)

The idiom "der Mühe wert" is equivalent to the English expression "worth the trouble." If one thinks of it as meaning "worthy of the trouble," it is easier to remember, because "Mühe" is in the genitive case. For this reason, choice (B) is incorrect, since "die Mühe" is not genitive. choice (C) appears to be genitive, but it is not, since "Mühe" is feminine. "Des" is the genitive definite article for the masculine and neuter. Choice (D) is incorrect because of the word order. In this expression, the noun comes first, unlike in the equivalent English expression.

17. (B)

"To be interested in" is rendered into German by "interessieren an" +dative, or "sich interessieren für" + accusative. Since "die Musik von Mozart" is in the accusative, the only possibility is "sich interessieren für." Choices (A) and (C) are not possible.

18. (C)

"Helfen" is a verb that takes a dative object. All of the pronouns listed here are accusative, except for "ihm."

19. (B)

In order to do this, you must be familiar with the idiom "sich in jemanden (accusative) verlieben." The English equivalent is "to fall in love with someone." Choice (A) does not exist. The word "beliebt" alone means "beloved" or "popular." Choice (C) is incorrect, because the object must be in the accusative case. "Mir" is the dative. In choice (D), everything is correct except the verb. "Geliebt" is the past participle of the verb "lieben," "to love" and does not fit here. One can say "Er hat mich geliebt." (He loved me.)

20. (D)

Missing here is a relative pronoun. In order to use relative pronouns, you must know two things: the gender of the word it refers to (antecendent) and how it is used in the relative clause. Here the antecedent is "Mann" and it is the direct object (accusative case) of the verb "sah." Except for the genitive forms (dessen, deren, dessen, deren) and the dative plural (denen), relative pronouns look like the definite article. Just as the masculine, definite article in the accusative case is "den," so is the relative pronoun. Choice (A) could be a relative pronoun, but it is the wrong case to fit here. Choice (B) could also be a relative pronoun, but it is the wrong gender for this relative clause. Choice (C) could also be a relative pronoun, but it is in the dative case.

21. (D)

In order to do this, you need to know that "auf" is a "two way" preposition. This means that it can either be followed by the dative or the accusative case. If motion toward a goal is described, as is the case here, the accusative case is used. The bottle was placed on the table. You also need to know that "Tisch" is masculine. Another way of looking at it is that "stellen" is a verb of motion. If the verb were "stehen," there would be no motion involved and the dative case would be used. For example" Die Flasche steht auf dem Tisch. (The bottle is on the table.)

This explains why choice (A) is incorrect. Choice (B) is wrong, because it is either the wrong case (nominative), or the wrong gender (femine, dative or genitive). Choice (C) can either be feminine nominative or accusative. Therefore, it is incorrect on all counts.

22. (B)

Definite time expressions such as this one, which means "the whole day" are in the accusative case. Choice (A) is incorrect, because it is in the nominative case. Choice (C) is the dative case. Choice (D) is the genitive case. There are time expressions in the genitive case, but they are indefinite time expressions, such as "eines Tages" (one day).

23. (A)

The interrogative "who" has three forms in German, depending upon its case. The case here is nominative. Therefore, "wer" is the correct form. Choice (B) does not fit, because it is not an interrogative form. Choice (C) is accusative. An example of its use would be:

Wen hast du gesehen? (Whom did you see?)

Choice (D) is dative. An example of its use is:

Wem hast du das Buch gegeben?
(To whom did you give the book?)

24. (B)

The idiom "nach Hause" is used after verbs or motion to mean "home." Choice (A) is used after other verbs and means "at home." For example: Er ist nicht zu Hause.
(He isn't at home.)

The prepositional phrase in choice (C) means "in the house" and doesn't fit here, because of the motion verb "kommen." Choice (D) is not possible. The preposition "nach" generally means "to" when followed by a proper name: Er fährt nach Berlin.
(He is driving to Berlin.)

25. (C)

"Kein" has the same endings as the indefinite article "ein." It is used to negate nouns without an article, as in this example. It also replaces "nicht" + "ein." For example:

Ich habe kein Buch von ihm gelesen.
(I haven't read a book by him.)

Choice (A) negates a verb. For example:

Ich habe das Buch nicht gelesen.
(I haven't read that book.)

Choice (B) is incorrect, because neuter, accusative ein-words have no ending. Choice (D) is used to answer a question in the negative.

26. (B)

"Gafallen" is a verb that takes a dative object. The best way to think of it is that it means "to be pleasing to." The person or thing that is pleasing is in the nominative case and the person to whom it is pleasing is in the dative case. In the example, "sein Haus" is nominative and "dir" is dative. The literal meaning is": "Is his house pleasing to you?" Since "dich" in choice (A), "sie," in choice (C) and "ihn" in choice (D) are all accusative, they do not fit.

27. (A)

This is a well-known proverbial saying in both English and German: "He who laughs last, laughs best." In the German version, "wer" is the subject of the verb "lacht." Choice (B) is incorrect, because it is accusative. Choice (C) is incorrect, because it is dative. Choice (D) means "where" and doesn't fit.

28. (B)

In order to answer this, you must know the verb "ankommen," which means "to arrive." There is also the verb "vorkommen," as in choice (A), but it means "to happen" and doesn't fit here. An example of its use:

Das Kommt oft vor.
(That happens often.)

Choices (C) and (D) are prepositions which need an object. Therefore, they do not fit. "An" in the test example is not a preposition, but a separabel prefix. It is part of the verb.

29. (B)

"Um...zu" is the German equivalent of "in order to." The expression "in Ordnung" given in (A) exists, but doesn't fit here. It means "in order." For example:

Seine Sachen sind in Ordnung.
(His things are in order)

The combinations in (C) and (D) do not exist.

30. (A)

After "etwas," an adjective can be turned into a neuter noun. It always ends in -es. Other examples are "etwas Gutes" (something good), "etwas Schünes" (something beautiful) etc. Choices (B), (C), and (D) all have the wrong ending.

31. (C)

An adjective used as a noun after "ein" has the same ending it would have if it were simply used as an adjective. "Ein Deutscher" is masculine, nominative in this sentence. Therefore, the adjective ending is -er. Choice (A) is incorrect, because it has no ending. As it stands, it refers to the language, German. For example:

Er Lernt Deutsch.
(He is learning German.)

Choice (B) would be correct if the article were "eine" (feminine, nominative or accusative). For example:

Eine Deutsche war bei uns zu Besuch.
(A German (woman) was visiting us.)

Choice (D) would be correct if the article were "einen" (masculine, accusative). For example:

Ich sah einen Deutschen.
(I saw a German (man).

32. (B)

Indefinite time expressions are in the genitive case. That is the case in this sentence, which means: "One day he came unexpectedly." Choice (A) is nominative and doesn't fit grammatically. Choice (C) is accusative and choice (D) is dative. Neither fit here.

33. (A)

When a relative pronoun is necessary and there is no specific word to which it refers, "was" is used. That is the case here. Choice (B) could also be used if "welcher" were in the accusative case. "Ich weiß nicht, welchen er meint" means "I don't know which one he means." The antecedent for "welchen" would have to be masculine. Choice (C) is also incorrect, because of its case. In order to be used here, it would have to be accusative.

"Ich weiß nicht, wen er meint" means "I don't know who he means." Choice (D) is in the dative case and could fit into this sentence only if the verb were changed, since "meinen" takes an accusative object.

34. (C)

To answer this question, you need to know that this is a reflexive verb (sich erinnern). With the first person singular pronoun, there are always two possibilities when the verb is reflexive. The reflexive can be either "mich" (accusative) or "mir" (dative). The accusative form is used when there is not another accusative object of the verb in the sentence. "Die Zeit" is the object of the preposition "an." Answer (D) would be possible in a sentence with an accusative object of the verb.

Example:	ICH wasche mir	die Hände.
	dat. reflexive	acc. object

Answer (A) would be the correct reflexive form for 3rd. person singular and plural (er, sie, es, sie) or for the formal you (Sie). "Selbst"is an intensifier and can be used in addition to the reflexive participle but not in place of it.

35. (D)

The exclamation point at the end of the sentence shows that an imperative form is missing. The preceding sentence shows that the imperative is being addressed to one person with whom the speaker is on a familiar basis. Therefore, you must decide which is the correct "du" imperative form of the verb "fahren." In order to eliminate (A), you must know that verbs which add an Umlaut to the stem of the "du" form in the present tense drop the Umlaut in the imperative. DU FÄHRST -> Fahre. Answer (B) is also incorrect, because the "du" imperative also drops the -st ending of the present tense. (C) would be correct, if the speaker were addressing more than one person with whom he is on a familiar basis. It is the "ihr" form of the imperative and would be correct had the sentence read: "Seid ihr verrückt?"

36. (A)

"Es gibt" corresponds to the english "there is/there are." It is always singular even when followed by a plural noun and translated "there are" into English. Since it is always singular, answer (B) is incorrect. Answer (C) translates literally as "there are," but "es sind" is a more specific statement than "es gibt" and would be inappropriate here. "Es gibt" refers to the existence of something or someone, as in the statement above. Perhaps the difference is best illustrated by these examples:

Es gibt weiße Mäuse.
(There are white mice.)
Es sind zwei weiße Mäuse in diesem Zimmer.
(There are two white mice in this room.)

The last possibility is least likely, since it neither fits the meaning of the sentence, which expresses merely the existence of people who like to play football, nor would it fit grammatically.

If the verb "to be" were possible at all here, it would have to be plural.

37. (B)

There are three words in German which correspond to the English word "when." They are "wann," "als," and "wenn." Of these three, the easiest is "wann." It is always used in questions, direct or indirect and in any tense. For example:

Wann kommst du?
Weiß du, wann du gekommen bist?

The next easiest is "als." It is always used in the past tense to express a one time past action. That is the case in the question. "Wenn" is the most difficult, because it can be used in any tense. When used in the past, it expresses a repeated past action. It often corresponds to the English "whenever." For example:

Wenn ich nach Deutschland fuhr, nahm ich immer meinen Hund mit.

(Whenever I went to Germany, I always took my dog along.)

Choice (D) means "although" and would not fit logically into the sentence.

38. (B)

"Immer noch" corresponds to "still" in English. Except for "immer nicht," which doesn't exist as a phrase, the other examples are legitimate, but do not fit into the context of the sentence. Choice (C) means "again and again." Choice (D) means "more and more." "Immer + a comparative, as in the last example corresponds to the English comparative construction "(more) and (more)."

Other examples: "immer schwerer" (more and more difficult)
"immer schöner" (more and more beautiful)
"immer billiger" (cheaper and cheaper)

39. (B)

This is a well-known legend and should cause no problems. However, in order to find the correct answer, it helps to know that the verb "entfernen" means "to remove." The verb used in the text, "befreien," means "to free" or "to liberate." The Pied-Piper did not want to free the city of the plague of children for nothing (umsonst) (A), or free it from rats in exchange for children (C), nor was it his original intention to lead the children out of the city (D).

40. (C)

The result of his playing was that the rats and mice followed him out of the city and drowned in the river. In the text, the verb meaning "to drown" (ertrinken) was used. In answer (C), the verb "umkommen" (to die) was used. It is true, as stated in question (A), that the citizens did not want to pay him, but that was not the result of his playing. They did not follow him into the next city, as stated in answer (B), but into the river. Answer (D) states that a lot of citizens threw themselves in the water and drowned.

41. (A)

The result of his success was not what he had expected. Rather than finally receiving his money (D), he went away disappointed (enttäuscht) and unhappy (unglücklich). It is true that the people did not want to pay him, it is not true that he received the money anyway (B). He then dressed as a hunter, but he did not shoot the citizens of the city (C).

42. (B)

As stated in the reading, this myth is often read in schools. However, this assertion is worded slightly differently than in answer (B). The text stated that it is a standard part of school instruction ("...gehört...zum Standardprogram des Schulunterrichts"). Answer (A) claims it is less well-known than other myths. Answer (C) asserts that the story has now been completely explained. This is not the case. Answer (D) says it has nothing to do with life in the 13th century. This is also not true. The story originated during the time in which Europe was plagued by rats and is probably based upon tales told about means of ridding cities of rats.

43. (A)

There are often problems between neighbors in large cities because of lack of space ("man hat wenig Platz"). In the text this idea is expressed as "das enge Zusammenleben." Literally translated, this means "narrow co-existence." We can hope that it is not true, as stated in answer (B), that people like to fight with each other. Needless to say, it can happen that one doesn't like one's neighbors (C), but this is not the reason given in this reading for the problems. We also cannot blame problems of co-existence upon animals fighting with each other as suggested in answer (D).

44. (B)

Fredi's neighbor complained because he made too much noise with his crowing, not because he ruined the construction machinery (A), or used it (D). It was the lawyer with wracked nerves ("entnervt"), not Fredi (B).

45. (C)

Fredi's punishment was unfair, because he had to be quiet longer than the construction machinery, with which the lawyer had compared him. Answer (A) is probably also true. Fredi's crowing was probably not as disturbing as the construction machinery, but this is not the reason given in the text for considering his treatment unfair. The same is true for answer (B). It might have been unfair to lock him in a stall, but this is not the reason given in the text. Answer (D) states his treatment was unfair because he was a rooster and not a piece of construction machinery. This might also be true, but is not based on the text.

46. (D)

The second trial was more favorable for Fredi, because he had to be quiet only between the hours of 10:00 AM and 7:00 PM, not between 8:00 PM and 8:00 AM. He could crow longer. The time for use of construction machines was not changed, as stated in (A). There was also no change in the life of Fredi's owner. He was always allowed to run free (B). It was never a question of Fredi's going away (C).

47. (D)

This reading is concerned with how one becomes a Rock Star in the German Democratic Republic ("im anderen Teil Deutschlands" = in the other part of Germany) and not in West-Germany (A), nor is it concerned with the general question of how to become a Rock Star (B). Although the reading states that Tamara Danz has become the German Tina Turner, it does not explain how one becomes a Tina Turner (C).

48. (A)

Tamara Danz wanted to study at the Berlin "Hochschule für Musik." It is not true that she only wanted to study German from the beginning (B). She was always interested in a career in music. She was not satisfied to appear as a singer "on the side" ("nebenbei") (C). She did not want to continue the student life she had led (D). After meeting other singers in Berlin, she decided to give up ("aufgeben") the student life.

49. (B)

She is happy that her application to study at the Berlin "Hochschule für Musik" was turned down, not disappointed ("enttäuscht") (A). She is not still hoping to be accepted there (C) and does not believe her hope will still be fulfilled (D).

50. (B)

She attended a small music school in Berlin, because one needs a professional certification (Berufsausweis") to practice any profession in the GDR. She did not attend that school because one must learn to play the piano, as stated in answer (A). The text does not state that piano and singing are in the foreground for her (C), but for the music school. She also did not attend it because it is better than the larger school (D).

51. (D)

Tamara Danz maintains that she had to teach herself everything she knows. Nevertheless, she does not consider education stupid ("blöd") (A), but says at least one doesn't become more stupid (blöder) from having received an education. Answer (B) maintains that one does indeed become more stupid from an education. Answer (C) says that one will learn from an education.

This idea is not expressed by Tamara Danz.

52. (A)

The next to last ("vorletzte") LP of her group is considered very important, a milestone ("Meilenstein") in GDR Rock history. Therefore, it is not considered insignificant ("Unbedeutend") (B), nor is it left unnoticed by critics (C). The group "Silly" was already no. 1 when this LP came out. It did not make them no. 1 (D).

53. (B)

It is her dream to perform in London, but she fears the English are not interested in German texts. She isn't worried about the music itself (A). Since it is her dream to perform in London, answer (C) (she doesn't think about it) and (D) (She only wants to visit West-Germany and Switzerland) are false.

54. (D)

In order to do this, you must first find the past participle at the end of the sentence. "Gegangen" is the past participle of the verb "gehen," which forms its perfect tenses with "sein." Most verbs in German form the perfect tenses with "haben." However, verbs which (1) have no object and (2) indicate a change of location or condition form the perfect tenses with "sein." Since "gehen" has no object and indicates a change of location, it forms its perfect tenses with "sein." That eliminates choices (A) and (B). Choice (C) is the imperfect of the verb "werden" and does not fit grammatically.

55. (D)

The masculine nominative adjective ending is -e when preceded by a "der-word." An easy way to remember this is that the masculine marker (-r) only appears once. When preceded by "der," it's already there. However, when preceded by "ein," it isn't and must be included: Ein junger Mann.... For this reason, choice (A) is wrong. Choice (B) is incorrect, because there is no adjective ending and all attributive adjectives (adjectives, which come before a noun) must have an ending. Choice (C) would be correct for the masculine accusative. Actually more adjectives end in -en than anything else. So, if forced to guess, -en is always the best guess, but it doesn't work here.

56. (A)

Definite time expressions like this one (every evening) are in the accusative case. Therefore choice (B) (nominative) is incorrect. Choice (C) is the wrong gender (neuter). Choice (D) is also the wrong gender (feminine).

57. (A)

"In" is a preposition which can be followed by either the accusative or the dative case. If it answers the question "Wo?" i.e. if it shows no motion, it is followed by the dative. If it answers the question "wohin?" i.e. if it shows motion, it is followed by the accusative. That is the case here. "Ins" is a contraction of "in das." Choice (B) has no article and is therefore wrong. The article in choice (C) is dative or genitive feminine. Choice (D) would be correct if "Theater" were masculine. Like most words of foreign origin in German, it is neuter.

58. (D)

"Hätte" is the Subjunctive II form of the verb "haben." In this sentence it is used as an auxiliary to form the past tense in the subjunctive. "Hätte er Zeit und Geld gahabt..." means "If he had had time and money...." The Subjunctive II is used here because it is an "if" ("wenn") clause with the "if" ("wenn") omitted. Such clauses are easy to recognize, because the verb is in first place and the punctuation shows that it is not a question. The formation of the Subjunctive II is based on the "wir" form of the imperfect tense. Irregular verbs with the vowels a, o or u add an Umlaut. Its endings are best remembered by the imperfect tense endings of "arbeiten" after the -t:

ich arbeitE	wir arbeitEN
du arbeitEST	ihr arbeitET
er arbeitET	sie arbeitEN

Therefore, to arrive at "hätte" in the example: Wir hatten-> er arbeitetE + Umlaut = hätte. The subjunctive II is used primarily to express contrary-to-fact conditions. Choice (A) is incorrect, because it is clear from the context of of the sentence that this is a contrary-to-fact condition (he had no time and money) and "hat" is not a subjunctive form. The same applies to choice (B). Since it has no umlaut, it is clear that it is not a subjunctive form. Choice (C) is either the "ich" form of the present tense of "haben" or the "ich" form of the present tense of "haben" or the "ich" and "er, sie, es" Subjunctive I form of "haben." Subjunctive I does not fit here, since Subjunctive I does not describe contrary-to-fact conditions. It is used in indirect discourse.

59. (A)

Choice (A) is the Subjunctive II form of the verb "sein." Here it is an auxiliary to form the past subjunctive II. Following the rules of formation stated above: wir waren-> er arbeitetE-> ware + Umlaut=wäre. Choice (B) is not a subjunctive form. Choice (C) is a subjunctive form, but the verb "bleiben" forms its perfect tenses with "sein." Choice (D) is not a subjunctive form.

60. (B)

This is an infinitive phrase formed with "um...zu," which means "in order to." Choice (A) means "and to write a novel" and does not fit into the context of the sentence. Choice (C) is not complete, because the "zu" is missing. Choice (D) has incorrect word order. In this, and in other infinitive phrases, the "zu" comes before the infinitive and the infinitive comes at the end of the phrase. Therefore, choice (D) has two mistakes in word order. It is a direct translation of English word order: in order to write a novel.

61. (B)

This is a comparative form. Most one syllable adjectives with the vowels a, o, or u add an umlaut in the comparative and superlative forms. That is the case with "alt." The next step in forming the comparative is to add the -er. Because this is an attributive adjective, it must also have an adjective ending. The ending is -e, because it is preceded by the indefinite article and is feminine nominative. Choice (A) is wrong, because there is no umlaut. Choice (C) is missing an umlaut and is also the wrong case (accusative) and gender (masculine). Choice (D) is missing the umlaut and the adjective ending.

62. (A)

"Die" is a relative pronoun. It is feminine, because it refers to "Dame" and nominative, because it is the subject of the relative clause. Choice (B) can only be used in questions. Choice (C) means "which" or "which one." The masculine -er ending eliminates it for use here. Choice (D) means "where" and does not fit the context.

63. (C)

Choice (C) is the imperfect of the verb "arbeiten." Choice (A) does not agree with the subject. It is the present tense "ich" form. Choices (B) and (D) are incorrect, because "arbeiten" forms its perfect tenses with "haben," they would be correct and would mean "worked" and "had worked."

64. (A)

"Ihre" means "here" in this sentence. Choice (B) would be possible as far as its meaning goes (his), but the -er ending is incorrect for the nominative case. The same is true for choice (C). Choice (D) would also be possible in meaning (his), but it needs an -e ending, since "Mutter" is feminine.

65. (C)

The preposition "bei" is followed by the dative case. For this reason, choices (A), (B), and (D) are incorrect. They are all accusative forms.

66. (A)

Before seasons the preposition "n" + the definite article is used. It is contracted to "im." Other examples: "im Herbst," "im Sommer," "im Winter." Since all the seasons are masculine, it is always "im." Choice (B) has the wrong gender (feminine). Choice (C) is the wrong preposition. Choice (D) is missing the definite article.

67. (B)

Since the word "viele" has no effect on adjective endings, this is an unpreceded adjective. The unpreceded adjective endings follow the pattern of the definite article, except in the genitive. Genitive endings are -en. In other cases, simply substitute the definite article to find out what the ending is. Here we would substitute "die" because "Tage" is plural. Therefore, the ending is -e. Choice (A) would be the correct plural adjective ending, if "Tage" were preceded by the definite article. Choice (C) is wrong, because it has no ending. All adjectives before nouns have an ending in German. Choice (D) would be the correct ending for a singular, unpreceded, masculine noun. For example:

Kalter Wein schmeckt mir.
(Cold wine tastes good to me.)

68. (C)

The simple past tense (imperfect) of the verb "stehen" is irregular: ich stand, du standest, er stand, wir standen, ihr standet, sie standen.

Choice (A) has confused the irregular form, which has no ending in the 3rd. person with a regular form like "arbeitete." Choice (B) doesn't exist. Choice (D) has failed to take into account the vowel change in the irregular verb and has simply treated it as a regular verb by adding the regular past tense ending -te to the stem.

69. (B)

"Neben" can be followed by an accusative or by a dative object, depending upon whether it indicates motion toward a goal (accusative), or no motion (dative). Here there is no motion, so the object is dative. Therefore, choice (A) is incorrect, because it is in the accusative. Choice (C) means "my" and does not fit. Choice (D) also means "my."

70. (B)

Here the conjugated verb "wollten" goes to the end of the clause, because of the subordinating conjunction "weil." Therefore choice (C) is wrong. Choice (A) is incorrect, because there is no "zu" before the infinitive when the conjugated verb is a modal. Choice (D) is incorrect, because the conjugated verb does not agree with the subject. It is the "ihr" form.

71. (D)

Bertolt Brecht was considered a sort of "artist-of-life" (he knew how to live), because hewas able to survive in difficult times ("er verstand es, sich in schwierigen Lagen durchzuschlagen"). This is stated slightly differently in (D): He knew how to save (retten) himself in difficult times. One is considered an artist ("Künstler"), but not a "Lebenskünstler" when one writes poetry (A). One is not considered a "Lebenskünstler" just because one is well-known ("bekannt") (B). He was not considered a "Lebenskünstler" because he beat ("schlagen") others, but because he could survive ("sich durchschlagen") (C).

72. (B)

Since Brecht was not satisfied with his grade, he circled a few correct answers as if they were incorrect. He did not throw his paper away ("wegwerfen") (A), or report his teacher to the police ("anzeigen") (C). He did not circle some incorrect answers, as if they were correct (D).

73. (D)

When Brecht showed the teacher his work again, the teacher thought he had made a mistake ("sich irren") and gave him a better grade. He did not say Brecht had made a mistake (A), nor did he say Brecht had no choice and must accept his grade (B). He also did not say Brecht's grade was satisfactory ("befriedigend") (C).

74. (A)

This story shows that Brecht was sly ("schlau"), but not always honest (ehrlich"). It does not show that he was a good ("brav" means "good" in the sense of "well-behaved"), obedient ("gehorsam") student (B). It certainly does not show that he was afraid of (Angst haben vor") his teacher (C). Furthermore, the story does not indicate that Brecht always got good grades without any effort (ohne Weiteres") (D).

75. (A)

The German got off the plane at the wrong place ("ist falsch ausgestiegen") because he did not understand enough English "(er konnte wenig Englisch"). He did not want to visit Bangor (B). "Besichtigen" means "to visit, tour, look around." The flight might have been too long (C), and he might have wanted to stretch his legs (D), but that was no reason to get off in Bangor, Maine when he wanted to go to San Francisco.

76. (B)

He got into a taxi because he wanted to go into the center of town, not because he was tired (A). He did not get into the taxi because he wanted to see a suburb of San Francisco, but because he thought he was already in a suburb (C). He also did not intend or want to travel 3000 miles by taxi (D).

77. (D)

The taxi-driver was perplexed, because they were already in the center of town, not because they were already in San Francisco (A). He was also not perplexed because the German had insulted him (B), or because he did not want to insult the German (C).

78. (B)

The German was astonished because he had not known that the plane had a stop-over ("Zwischenlandung") before landing in San Francisco, not because the taxi driver did not want to go, or because he did not want to visit San Francisco after all (C). The taxi driver did not want to drive 3000 miles in 4 hours (D).

79. (A)

The German was invited everywhere. He did not find the hospitality in Bangor unbearable ("unausstehlich") (B), nor did he fly on to San Francisco immediately (C). He planned to return to Bangor next year, not to San Francisco. (D).

80. (B)

The story shows what can happen when one has not mastered a language ("eine Sprache beherrschen" = to master a language), not what can happen when one goes to San Francisco (A). It also does not show what happens when one gets off a plane (C), or when one asks a taxi-driver something (D).

THE COLLEGE BOARD ACHIEVEMENT TEST IN

GERMAN

TEST III

THE COLLEGE BOARD ACHIEVEMENT TEST IN

GERMAN

ANSWER SHEET

1. Ⓐ Ⓑ Ⓒ Ⓓ Ⓔ
2. Ⓐ Ⓑ Ⓒ Ⓓ Ⓔ
3. Ⓐ Ⓑ Ⓒ Ⓓ Ⓔ
4. Ⓐ Ⓑ Ⓒ Ⓓ Ⓔ
5. Ⓐ Ⓑ Ⓒ Ⓓ Ⓔ
6. Ⓐ Ⓑ Ⓒ Ⓓ Ⓔ
7. Ⓐ Ⓑ Ⓒ Ⓓ Ⓔ
8. Ⓐ Ⓑ Ⓒ Ⓓ Ⓔ
9. Ⓐ Ⓑ Ⓒ Ⓓ Ⓔ
10. Ⓐ Ⓑ Ⓒ Ⓓ Ⓔ
11. Ⓐ Ⓑ Ⓒ Ⓓ Ⓔ
12. Ⓐ Ⓑ Ⓒ Ⓓ Ⓔ
13. Ⓐ Ⓑ Ⓒ Ⓓ Ⓔ
14. Ⓐ Ⓑ Ⓒ Ⓓ Ⓔ
15. Ⓐ Ⓑ Ⓒ Ⓓ Ⓔ
16. Ⓐ Ⓑ Ⓒ Ⓓ Ⓔ
17. Ⓐ Ⓑ Ⓒ Ⓓ Ⓔ
18. Ⓐ Ⓑ Ⓒ Ⓓ Ⓔ
19. Ⓐ Ⓑ Ⓒ Ⓓ Ⓔ
20. Ⓐ Ⓑ Ⓒ Ⓓ Ⓔ
21. Ⓐ Ⓑ Ⓒ Ⓓ Ⓔ
22. Ⓐ Ⓑ Ⓒ Ⓓ Ⓔ
23. Ⓐ Ⓑ Ⓒ Ⓓ Ⓔ
24. Ⓐ Ⓑ Ⓒ Ⓓ Ⓔ
25. Ⓐ Ⓑ Ⓒ Ⓓ Ⓔ
26. Ⓐ Ⓑ Ⓒ Ⓓ Ⓔ
27. Ⓐ Ⓑ Ⓒ Ⓓ Ⓔ
28. Ⓐ Ⓑ Ⓒ Ⓓ Ⓔ
29. Ⓐ Ⓑ Ⓒ Ⓓ Ⓔ
30. Ⓐ Ⓑ Ⓒ Ⓓ Ⓔ
31. Ⓐ Ⓑ Ⓒ Ⓓ Ⓔ
32. Ⓐ Ⓑ Ⓒ Ⓓ Ⓔ
33. Ⓐ Ⓑ Ⓒ Ⓓ Ⓔ
34. Ⓐ Ⓑ Ⓒ Ⓓ Ⓔ
35. Ⓐ Ⓑ Ⓒ Ⓓ Ⓔ
36. Ⓐ Ⓑ Ⓒ Ⓓ Ⓔ
37. Ⓐ Ⓑ Ⓒ Ⓓ Ⓔ
38. Ⓐ Ⓑ Ⓒ Ⓓ Ⓔ
39. Ⓐ Ⓑ Ⓒ Ⓓ Ⓔ
40. Ⓐ Ⓑ Ⓒ Ⓓ Ⓔ
41. Ⓐ Ⓑ Ⓒ Ⓓ Ⓔ
42. Ⓐ Ⓑ Ⓒ Ⓓ Ⓔ
43. Ⓐ Ⓑ Ⓒ Ⓓ Ⓔ
44. Ⓐ Ⓑ Ⓒ Ⓓ Ⓔ
45. Ⓐ Ⓑ Ⓒ Ⓓ Ⓔ
46. Ⓐ Ⓑ Ⓒ Ⓓ Ⓔ
47. Ⓐ Ⓑ Ⓒ Ⓓ Ⓔ
48. Ⓐ Ⓑ Ⓒ Ⓓ Ⓔ
49. Ⓐ Ⓑ Ⓒ Ⓓ Ⓔ
50. Ⓐ Ⓑ Ⓒ Ⓓ Ⓔ
51. Ⓐ Ⓑ Ⓒ Ⓓ Ⓔ
52. Ⓐ Ⓑ Ⓒ Ⓓ Ⓔ
53. Ⓐ Ⓑ Ⓒ Ⓓ Ⓔ
54. Ⓐ Ⓑ Ⓒ Ⓓ Ⓔ
55. Ⓐ Ⓑ Ⓒ Ⓓ Ⓔ
56. Ⓐ Ⓑ Ⓒ Ⓓ Ⓔ
57. Ⓐ Ⓑ Ⓒ Ⓓ Ⓔ
58. Ⓐ Ⓑ Ⓒ Ⓓ Ⓔ
59. Ⓐ Ⓑ Ⓒ Ⓓ Ⓔ
60. Ⓐ Ⓑ Ⓒ Ⓓ Ⓔ
61. Ⓐ Ⓑ Ⓒ Ⓓ Ⓔ
62. Ⓐ Ⓑ Ⓒ Ⓓ Ⓔ
63. Ⓐ Ⓑ Ⓒ Ⓓ Ⓔ
64. Ⓐ Ⓑ Ⓒ Ⓓ Ⓔ
65. Ⓐ Ⓑ Ⓒ Ⓓ Ⓔ
66. Ⓐ Ⓑ Ⓒ Ⓓ Ⓔ
67. Ⓐ Ⓑ Ⓒ Ⓓ Ⓔ
68. Ⓐ Ⓑ Ⓒ Ⓓ Ⓔ
69. Ⓐ Ⓑ Ⓒ Ⓓ Ⓔ
70. Ⓐ Ⓑ Ⓒ Ⓓ Ⓔ
71. Ⓐ Ⓑ Ⓒ Ⓓ Ⓔ
72. Ⓐ Ⓑ Ⓒ Ⓓ Ⓔ
73. Ⓐ Ⓑ Ⓒ Ⓓ Ⓔ
74. Ⓐ Ⓑ Ⓒ Ⓓ Ⓔ
75. Ⓐ Ⓑ Ⓒ Ⓓ Ⓔ
76. Ⓐ Ⓑ Ⓒ Ⓓ Ⓔ
77. Ⓐ Ⓑ Ⓒ Ⓓ Ⓔ
78. Ⓐ Ⓑ Ⓒ Ⓓ Ⓔ
79. Ⓐ Ⓑ Ⓒ Ⓓ Ⓔ
80. Ⓐ Ⓑ Ⓒ Ⓓ Ⓔ

GERMAN TES

4.

PART A

Time: 1 Hour
80 Questions

DIRECTIONS: Each of the sentences in this part has a blank space indicating that a word or phrase has been omitted. From the four choices select the ONE that, when inserted in the sentence, fits grammatically and logically with the sentence as a whole. Then blacken the corresponding space on the answer sheet.

1. Dieser Rennfahrer fuhr wieder _______ .

   (A) dem schnellsten

   (B) am schnellen

   (C) schnellsten

   (D) am schnellsten

2. Ich stehe schon stundenlang draußen im Schnee, und _____.

   (A) ich bin kalt!

   (B) mir ist kalt!

   (C) ich bin heiß!

   (D) ich habe heiß!

3. Wir fuhren mit dem neuen Wagen ______ See.

   (A) an den

   (B) auf den

   (C) nach dem

   (D) in den

Weil das Buch und der Film sehr langweilig waren, nehmen wir an, daß ____ das Buch ____ der Film sehr interessant gewesen waren.

(A) weder ... noch

(B) entweder ... oder

(C) entweder ... noch

(D) weder ... oder

5. Euer heute morgen ____ Buch war eine schöne Überraschung.

(A) angekommene

(B) angekommener

(C) angekommenes

(D) angekommenen

6. Wir hörten überhaupt nichts, ____ er sagte.

(A) das

(B) was

(C) welches

(D) dessen

7. Wenn Maria _____, würde sie ja auch staunen.

(A) dorthingehe

(B) dorthingeht

(C) dorthinging

(D) dorthinginge

8. _______ Mittagessen gibt es Fisch und Kartoffeln.

(A) Für

(B) Zu

(C) Zum

(D) Am

9. Robert bekommt ein neues Radio entweder _____ Geburtstag oder _____ Weihnachten.

(A) für ... für

(B) vor ... bei

(C) zum ... zu

(D) am ... an

10. Paul hat die Mutter den Weg entlang kommen _____.

(A) sehen

(B) gesehen

(C) sieht

(D) sah

11. Wir fragten ihn, aber er ______ nicht.

(A) klingelte

(B) sagte

(C) eswiderte

(D) lenkte

12. Ich wasche _____ die Hände.

(A) sich

(B) mein

(C) mir

(D) mich

13. Der alte Mann war _____.

(A) totmüde

(B) todmüde

(C) totenmüde

(D) todesmüde

14. Meine drei _______ merken nicht, wie sehr ich sie liebe.

(A) Hund

(B) Hunde

(C) Hunden

(D) Hünde

15. Die zwölf _______ im Park wurden frisch gestrichen.

(A) Bänke

(B) Bänken

(C) Banke

(D) Banken

16. Wir haben hier eine Nummer, eine Ziffer, und diese Nummer ist _______ Fünf.

(A) eines

(B) einer

(C) ein

(D) eine

17. Paula hat das Auto gefahren, _______ Tür kaputt ist.

(A) wessen

(B) das

(C) des

(D) dessen

18. Der Kranke wurde auch _______ über 100 Pillen nicht geheilt.

(A) durch

(B) von

(C) bei

(D) mit

19. Dieses neue Auto ist _______ als das alte Auto.

(A) schön

(B) schöner

(C) mehr schön

(D) mehr schöner

20. Sie wünscht, daß sie eih neues Auto kaufen _______.

(A) kann

(B) kannte

(C) konnte

(D) könnte

21. Während _________, aß er viel Schokalade.

(A) die Film

(B) dem Film

(C) des Films

(D) der Film

22. Wenn Herr Huber meint, daß er morgen um 11 Uhr vorbeikomme, dann besucht er mich also morgen _____.

(A) früh.

(B) vormittag.

(C) nachmittag.

(D) mittag.

23. Um 19 Uhr essen wir ______.

(A) Abend.

(B) Abendessen.

(C) zu Abend.

(D) zum Abendessen.

24. ______ heißt Ihr Vater?

(A) Wie

(B) Was

(C) Wo

(D) Wessen

25. Ilse und Ingrid ______ gestern arbeiten.

(A) mussen

(B) müssen

(C) müßten

(D) mußten

26. Der Arzt kommt zum Kranken _____ er kann.

(A) sobald

(B) so bald

(C) so bald als

(D) so bald wie

27. Er hat ein "A" bekommen, weil er an dem Tag vor der Prüfung sehr fleißig ______ hat.

(A) studiert

(B) gearbeitet

(C) geschlafen

(D) gespielt

28. Der Chef hat uns geschrieben, daß Frau Hansel momentan nicht sehr fleißig ______.

(A) arbeiten

(B) arbeitet

(C) arbeite

(D) arbeitest

29. Der Politiker bestand darauf, daß er gestern tatsächlich dahingefahren ———!

(A) sei

(B) sein

(C) ist

(D) hat

30. Obwohl Herr Schmidt der jungen Inge oft finanziell half, ... Inge den Herrn Schmidt nie.

(A) konnte

(B) kennte

(C) kannte

(D) könnte

31. Miriam fährt nächste Woche ... Frankreich.

(A) nach

(B) in

(C) zu

(D) an

32. Die … Kinder klingen schön.

(A) singen

(B) singenen

(C) singend

(D) singenden

33. Ich sagte dem …, daß es die Flugkarte des … sei.

(A) Pilot … Student

(B) Pilot … Students

(C) Pilots … Students

(D) Piloten … Studenten

34. Als Hans in New York war, hatte er Angst, die Unterführung

(A) zu fressen.

(B) nach fressen.

(C) zu benutzen.

(D) nach gebrauchen.

35. Du holst … schnell ein Programm.

(A) dir

(B) dich

(C) sich

(D) euch

36. … er uns das gestern gesagt, dann wären wir nicht sofort abgefahren.

(A) Hat

(B) Hatte

(C) Hätte

(D) Wäre

37. Wenn er gestern abend gesungen hätte, dann … wir langer geblieben.

(A) waren

(B) wären

(C) hatten

(D) hätten

38. Paula kann nicht mitkommen, denn …

(A) sie ist krank

(B) ist sie krank

(C) sie krank ist

(D) ist krank

PART B

DIRECTIONS: Read the following passages carefully for comprehension. Each passage is followed by a number of incomplete statements or questions. Select the completion or answer that is best according to the passage and blacken the corresponding space on the answer sheet.

Ich bin für alle Tag und Nacht da. Ich koche, bediene, und spüle mindestens dreimal am Tageab, jeden Tag der Woche. Ich bin Putzfrau, Betreuer, Krankenschwester, Lehrerin, Beraterin, Sekretärin, alles in einem. Wenn ich nicht in der Küche bin, so bin ich im Waschraum mit der Wäsche oder im Lebensmittelgeschäft, oder ich sitze im Auto als Chauffeur und bringe die Kinder zum Spielplatz, zur Geburtstagsparty, zum Arzt oder Zahnarzt, und wer weiß, sonst noch wohin. Meine Dienststunden sind nicht von 9 bis 5, sondern sie haben kein Ende, weil meine Arbeit kein Ende hat. Sie fängt immer wieder neu an. Dabei verdiene ich keinen Pfennig und nur selten ein "Danke schön." Die Personen, für die ich das alles mache, sind nicht besonders dankbar, sie nehmen alles im Kauf.

39. Was bin ich?

    (A) Ärztin

    (B) Dienstmädchen

    (C) Hausfrau

    (D) Verkäuferin

40. Diese Dame ist offenbar sehr

    (A) verschwenderisch.

    (B) faul.

    (C) zerstreut.

    (D) fleißig.

41. Fur diese Arbeit wird sie

(A) nicht bezahlt.

(B) schlecht bezahlt.

(C) gut bezahlt.

(D) schwer bestraft.

42. Wo arbeitet die Dame am meisten?

(A) im Geschäft

(B) im Auto

(C) zu Hause

(D) in der Schule

43. Wer sind die Personen, die "nicht besonders dankbar" seien?

(A) Angestellte

(B) Patienten

(C) Arbeitskollegen

(D) Familienmitglieder

44. Diese Personen halten die Arbeit der Dame für selbstverständlich. Das heißt, daß sie

(A) für den Dienst dieser Dame bezahlen.

(B) die Leistung der Dame ohne weiteres erwarten.

(C) mit der Hausarbeit helfen.

(D) sehr dankbar für die fieberhafte Tätigkeit der Dame sind und sich täglich sehr dankbar zeigen.

Er steht hinter dem Haus und ist von einem Zaun eingeschloßen. Hier wachsen drei Bäume, viel Gras, und sogar im sommer Gemüse und Obst. Er braucht viel Arbeit im Frühling und im Sommer; z.B., man muß dann mähen und Beete gießen. Aber deshalb ist alles auch friedlich, schön, und bunt. Dann macht er uns viel Freude. Die Kinder spielen dort, Peter, z.B., setzt sich oft auf die Schaukel und läßt sich die Sonne auf die Nase scheinen. Und wir essen dort ab und zu an einem Tisch, oder der Vater sitzt in einem Stuhl und tut nichts und erholt sich. Die Vögel besuchen uns, besonders die frechen Spatzen.

Im Winter wird er vom Schnee bedeckt.

45. Es ist unser

(A) Haus.

(B) Park.

(C) Gras.

(D) Garten.

46. Was könnte hier "bunt" sein?

(A) der Vater

(B) der Schnee

(C) die Blumen

(D) der Rasen

47. Ein Spatz ist ein

(A) Schnee.

(B) Gartengerät.

(C) Vogel.

(D) Insekt.

48. Der Vater erholt sich sehr wahrscheinlich von

(A) den Ferien.

(B) der Arbeit.

(C) seinem Mittagsschläfchen.

(D) der Sonne.

49. "Er macht uns viel Freude" heißt, daß

(A) es uns Spaß macht.

(B) er uns viel Kummer bringt.

(C) es viel Arbeit bedarf.

(D) es uns nur Sorgen macht.

Unser Sonnenschein und treuer Kamerad,
unser unvergeßlicher Fritz,
ist heute im Alter von knapp 8 Jahren für immer friedlich eingeschlafen. Bis zum letzten Atemzug hat er uns nur Freude und Anhänglichkeit geschenkt. Jeder, der ihn kannte, hat ihn lieb gewonnen. Er hinterließ zwei traurige Herzen und viele Freunde.

In aller Stille haben wir ihn zur letzten Ruhe gebettet. Möge der liebe gott Deine kleine, reine Seele bei sich aufnehmen und behüten, lieber Fritz. Wir behalten Dich in glücklicher Erinnerung.

50. Der "Kamerad" ist sehr wahrscheinlich ein(e)

(A) Mann

(B) Teddybär

(C) Puppe

(D) Haustier

51. Was ist dem Kamerad passiert?

(A) Er hat diese Leute verlassen und wohnt jetzt irgendwoanders.

(B) Nichts ist ihm passiert.

(C) Er ist gestorben.

(D) Er ist für die Nacht schlafengegangen.

52. Der Kamerad wohnte bei

(A) zwei Personen, möglicherweise einem Ehepaar.

(B) einem alten, traurigen Mann.

(C) einer alten, traurigen Dame.

(D) einer Familie mit Kindern.

53. Die Leute sind … , daß der Kamerad nun weg ist.

(A) froh

(B) traurig

(C) unbekümmert

(D) wütend

54. Der Kamerad ist

(A) eine Katze.

(B) ein Pferd.

(C) ein Hund.

(D) ein Drache.

55. Der Kamerad wurde

(A) vergessen.

(B) ausgestopft.

(C) weggeworfen.

(D) begraben.

PART C

DIRECTIONS: The sentences below contain blank spaces indicating omissions in the text. Below each blank are four choices. Select the choice that is grammatically correct in the context and blacken the corresponding space on the answer sheet. Be sure to read the sentences first.

Wissen Sie, einige … Freunde von … ,

56. (A) gute
(B) gutes
(C) gutem
(D) guten

57. (A) Sie
(B) Ihnen
(C) du
(D) dir

… ich in Deutschland besucht habe, fuhren voriges Jahr … .

58. (A) die
(B) deren
(C) denen
(D) den

59. (A) nach Schweiz
(B) in Schweiz
(C) in die Schweiz
(D) in der Schweiz

Sie erwiesen Paula ... dreimal, ... aber nur einmal;

60.	(A) diese Ehre	61.	(A) ich
	(B) dieser Ehre		(B) mir
	(C) diesen Ehre		(C) mich
	(D) dieses Ehre		(D) mein

sie hat also diese Auszeichnung ... erhalten als ...

62.	(A) oft	63.	(A) ich
	(B) öfter		(B) mir
	(C) öfters		(C) mich
	(D) öfterer		(D) mein

Warum schreiben sie immer über ... Onkel? Alles, ... sie

64.	(A) ihre	65.	(A) dessen
	(B) ihrer		(B) welches
	(C) ihrem		(C) was
	(D) ihren		(D) das

in ... Brief geschrieben haben, hat immer etwas ..., von dem alten Kerl, zu tun.

66.	(A) der	67.	(A) von ihm
	(B) des		(B) davon
	(C) dem		(C) von ihn
	(D) den		(D) darüber

Jürgen ist ein ... Student. ... wird er ... ,

68.		69.		70.	
(A)	nette	(A)	Ein Tag	(A)	Arzt
(B)	netter	(B)	Einen Tag	(B)	ein Arzt
(C)	nettem	(C)	Einem Tag	(C)	einer Arzt
(D)	netten	(D)	Eines Tages	(D)	einen Arzt

denn er möchte ... Menschen helfen.

71. (A) andere
    (B) anderer
    (C) anderen
    (D) anderem

PART D

DIRECTIONS: Read the following passages carefully for comprehension. Each passage is followed by a number of incomplete statements or questions. Select the completion or answer that is best according to the passage and blacken the corresponding space on the answer sheet.

Der Löwe, der Tiger, und der Wolf haben starke Zähne und scharfe Krallen. Der Elefant hat Stoßzähne und einen Rüssel. Der Stier, das Nashorn, und der Büffel haben Hörner. Die Schildkröte hat einen Panzer, der Igel Stacheln, manche Schlangen Gift, und manche Insekten Tarnung. Anderen Tieren, wie dem Hasen und der Gazelle, hat die Natur ihre Schnelligkeit gegeben.

72. Es ist hier über ... der Tiere geschrieben.

(A) das Temperament

(B) die Waffen und den Schutz

(C) die Größe und Geschwindigkeit

(D) das Aussehen

73. Der Hase schützt sich gegen Feinde, indem er

(A) stark beißen kann.

(B) einen ekelhaften Geruch abgeben kann.

(C) giftig ist.

(D) geschwind weglaufen kann.

74. Welches Tier hat keine Hörner?

(A) Das Stier

(B) Das Nashorn

(C) Der Elefant

(D) Der Büffel

Die Bürger im Dorfe Schilda sind sehr intelligente Leute. Wir sehen das, als wir zuschauen, wie sie ihr Rathaus bauen. Sie holten das Bauholz fürs Haus aus einem nahen Wald, schleppten die Stämme über den Berg, und auf der anderen Seite des Berges trugen sie sie wieder hinunter. Da sagte plötzlich ein Schildbürger, "Warum tragen wir die schweren Stämme hinunter? Wir können sie ja hinunterrollen lassen. Das wäre einfacher und schneller." So holten sie alle Stämme [aus dem Dorf hinaus (die sie vorhin hinuntergetragen hatten) und trugen sie wieder auf den Berg hinauf]. Dann rollten sie die Stämme ins Dorf hinunter.

Danach bauten sie ihr Rathaus. Als sie damit fertig waren, merkten sie, daß es im Rathaus sehr dunkel war. (Es hatte keine Fenster.) "Wie bekommen wir Licht in das Haus hinein?" fragten sie sich. "Ganz einfach," sagte einer, "Wir müssen das Dach entfernen, dann haben wir genügend Licht." So entfernten sie das Dach und sie hatten viel Licht im Innern des Baues. Die Schildbürger waren glücklich und stolz auf ihre Klugheit.

75. Der Autor nennt die Schildbürger "klug." Damit will er ... sein.

(A) ehrlich

(B) todernst

(C) albern

(D) sarkastisch

76. Schilda ist ein(e)

(A) Dorf.

(B) Stadt.

(C) Großstadt.

(D) Land.

77. Das zweite "sie" im dritten Satz. "...trugen sie sie wieder hinunter," bezieht sich auf die

(A) Schildbürger.

(B) Stämme.

(C) Berge.

(D) die Seite des Berges.

78. Die Erzählung gibt uns hier ... Beispiel(e) der Dummheit der Schildbürger.

(A) kein

(B) ein

(C) zwei

(D) drei

79. Die Stämme fürs Rathaus kommen von

(A) einem Möbelgeschäft.

(B) einer Betonfabrik.

(C) dem Dorf Schilda.

(D) Bäumen.

80. Wir wissen, daß die Schildbürger ... für das Rathaus vergessen hatten.

(A) das Dach

(B) die Wände

(C) die Fenster

(D) den Boden

THE COLLEGE BOARD ACHIEVEMENT TEST IN GERMAN

TEST III

ANSWER KEY

1.	D	21.	C	41.	A	61.	B
2.	B	22.	B	42.	C	62.	B
3.	A	23.	C	43.	D	63.	A
4.	A	24.	A	44.	B	64.	D
5.	C	25.	D	45.	D	65.	C
6.	B	26.	A	46.	C	66.	C
7.	D	27.	B	47.	C	67.	A
8.	C	28.	C	48.	B	68.	B
9.	C	29.	A	49.	A	69.	D
10.	A	30.	C	50.	D	70.	A
11.	C	31.	A	51.	C	71.	C
12.	C	32.	D	52.	A	72.	B
13.	B	33.	D	53.	B	73.	D
14.	B	34.	C	54.	C	74.	C
15.	A	35.	A	55.	D	75.	D
16.	D	36.	C	56.	A	76.	A
17.	D	37.	B	57.	B	77.	B
18.	A	38.	A	58.	A	78.	C
19.	B	39.	C	59.	C	79.	D
20.	D	40.	D	60.	A	80.	C

GERMAN TEST III DETAILED EXPLANATIONS OF ANSWERS

1. (D)

The superlative form of an adjective, used when comparing predicate adjectives or when comparing adverbs, has an "am" before the adjective/adverb and has the suffix "sten":

schnell: am schellsten billig: am billigsten

Most superlatives have umlauts also (e.g.: arm, am ärmsten). But watch for the usual irregular forms (e.g.: viel, am meisten; not am vielsten).

2. (B)

In general, "sein" used with the predicate nominative indicates a more or less permanent state (Ich bin dumm/klein), not a temporary one. Thus, here and in similar situations, choice A ("Ich bin kalt") is incorrect. Instead, use the dative without a grammatical subject: "Mir ist kalt/warm/heiß" and never "Ich bin kalt/warm/heiß" for describing such temporary conditions.

3. (A)

Prepositions are tricky to use in any language. The English "to" is no exception in German. Generally, "to" is "an" when going toward furniture or bodies of water: "Er geht an den Tisch/den See." "Zu" would also be used here. The German "in" is used for the English "into"; i.e., when going to (into) an interior, such as a room. Thus, "Wir fuhren in den See." would mean to drive into the lake, which is unlikely.

"Auf" can mean "to" in some expressions ("Er geht auf die Bude/ Bank/Uni, but it generally means "on", not "to".

4. (A)

Neither (weder) the film nor (noch) the book was interesting according to the critic. "Entweder...oder" means "either...or" and does not make sense here. The other choices do not exist in German.

5. (C)

After the possessive pronouns (mein, dein, etc.) the following descriptive adjective takes the primary ("strong") endings: "Mein altes Buch", "euer altes Buch," etc. The use of the extended adjective construction makes no difference: "Mein/Euer angekommenes Buch", etc.

6. (B)

"Was" must be used as the relative pronoun for all indefinite pronoun antecedents or when referring to an entire clause (idea). Thus, "was" follows "alles", "nichts", "vieles", "etwas", etc. "Alles/ Nichts/Vieles, was er sagt, ist mir sehr klar." In addition, it can follow an entire clause: "Sie gab mir ein schönes Buch, was mich sehr freute." "Was" refers back to the entire clause here, to the entire idea, that I was pleased that she gave me something.

7. (D)

The general subjunctive (subjunctive II) is used for unreal conditions, i.e., situations contrary-to-fact. It can deal with the future, present, or past. For weak verbs: To form the future and present contrary-to-fact (unreal) condition, use the indicative past tense form (e.g.: bezahlte, bezahltest, bezahlte,bezahlten, bezahltet, bezahlten). The general subjunctive form of a strong verb is achieved by adding the suffixes -e, -est, -e, -en, -et, and -en to the imperfect form of the third person singular; e.g.: ging (imperfect third person singular) + suffixes = ginge, gingest, ginge, gingen, ginget, gingen."Wenn Maria dorthinginge, würde sie ja auch staunen." If Maria would go there, she would also be suprised.

If a strong verb has an "a, o, (or) u" in its imperfect stem, an umlaut is needed; e.g., äße, äßest, äße, äßen, äßet, äßen: "Wenn die Kinder nicht so viel äßen, so wären sie nicht so dick." If the children would not eat so much, then they would not be so fat.

8. (C)

The word "for", when used in such phrases as "for breakfast" or "for lunch", is translated as "zu" in German. The definite article of the meal is also used, and is combined with "zu" to form the contraction "zum" (zu and dem). "Zu" is used alone when it is followed by a holiday, as in "zu Ostern" (for Easter); no article is needed.

9. (C)

This is the same as the previous exam item (number 8, above) in that one again needs to determine which preposition to use for which situation. "For" cannot always be translated as "für" and "to" cannot always be translated as "zu". Thus, doing or receiving something for Easter, Christmas, New Year's, one's birthday, etc. or being on or going for a holiday or vacation is not expressed with "für", but with just about every German preposition except "für": use "zu" for the holidays (zu Ostern/Weihnachten/Silvester), "zum" for one's birthday (zum Geburstag). The other choices are incorrect, because certain phrases call for certain prepositions, and in this case "zun" and "zu" are needed.

10. (A)

"Hören, sehen, lassen, helfen, heißen" (command), and the modal auxiliaries do not take the past participle (gehört, gesehen, etc.) but their infinitive form whenever used in the present perfect and past perfect tenses. Since we then have two infinitives, it is called appropriately the "double infinitive": Paul hat ihn kommen sehen; er hat es gestern liegen lassen; ich habe nie kommen wollen (a modal); and so on.

11. (C)

Of the choices that are given, only "erwiderte" (he replied) makes sense in the context of the sentence. The other choices do not: ...aber er klingelte uns nicht. (...but he did not ring (a bell) us.) ...aber er bratete uns nicht. (... but he did not roast us.) ...aber er lenkte uns nicht. (...but he did not steer us.)

Although the other choices are grammatically correct, they do not make as much sense as choice (C).

12. (C)

The dative reflexive pronouns (mir, dir, sich, uns, euch, and sich) are used when referring to parts of the body or clothing with the definite article (where English uses the possessive). This dative reflexive pronoun is used only if there is a direct object in the sentence ("Hände", in this sentence) and shows that the accusative object belongs to the subject of the sentence.

13. (B)

Compound adjectives use the stem "tod-" (todmüde, todernst, todsicher, etc.) or "toten-" (totenblaß, totenstill, etc.), but verbs use "tot-" (totlachen, totschlagen, etc.).

14. (B)

Mastering German plurals is not easy because the rules are few or they are confusing. The tendency among English-speaking people is to want to add "en" to words ending in consonants, but that is only one way to pluralize nouns (e.g., Held, Helden; Übung, Übungen). Another way, too often forgotten, is to simply add "e" to the final consonant. Thus the plural of "Hund" is "Hunde". Other words that pluralize by adding only "e" are "Tag" (Tage), "Monat" (Monate), and "Jahr" (Jahre). Adding "en" to them is incorrect (except in the plural dative case, of course).

15. (A)

Be careful of homonyms whose singular forms sometimes differ in gender (der Band (volume), das Band (band, ribbon, tape), and those whose singular forms are of the same gender ("die Bank" for "bench" and "bank"). These homonyms will often have different plural forms: der Band, die Bande; das Band, die Bänder/Bande (depending on meaning). The plural here is "Bänke" (benches), not "Banken" (banks (for money)). Another example: der Schild, die Schilde (shield(s)); das Schild, die Schilder (sign(s), doorplate(s)).

16. (D)

"We have a number, a numeral, here, and it is a five." Cardinal numbers have a feminine gender when used as nouns. Likewise: "Das Haus hat eine Sieben"; "er ist eine Null": "The house has a (figure) seven"; he is a nobody (a zero, a nothing)".

17. (D)

"Paula drove the car whose (dessen) door is broken." The relative pronoun in the genetive is "deren" (feminine and plural reference) or "dessen" (masc. and neuter reference). "Dessen" is used in this sentence because it refers to "das Auto", a singular, neuter form.

18. (A)

"Von" is used in passive sentence structures when the agent of the action that is performed on the subject is a person. The agent is then in its dative form. "Durch" is used when the agent is not a person. The agent is then in its accusative form. "Bei" and "mit" do not indicate agents of action.

19. (B)

When comparing two things, add "-er" to the adverb/adjective stem; monosyllabic adjectives that have an "a", "o", or "u" in their stems are usually umlauted (alt, älter). Adjectives that have "au" are not umlauted (laut, lauter). Adverbs/adjectives never form the comparative with a "mehr" in front, not as in English, in which one says "more beautiful", rather than "beautifuller", "more suitable" and not "suitabler", etc. Thus (here): "more beautiful" is "schöner".

20. (D)

"She wishes that she could buy a new car."

Since the subordinate clause represents something that is contrary to fact, the subjunctive form of "können" must be used. "Kann" is the present indicative form, "kannte" does not exist, and "konnte" is the imperfect indicative form.

21. (C)

The object of a phrase that is begun by "während" (during) is in the genitive case. "Die Film" does not exist in German ("Film" is masculine), "dem Film" is in the dative case, and "der Film" is nominative.

22. (B)

The time between about 9 a.m. and noon is "vormittag", "Morgen früh" is early morning (before about 9 a.m.). After 12 noon it is "nachmittag", the afternoon. "Mittag" is noontime.

23. (C)

When speaking of eating lunch or supper, do not use the word "essen" twice in the same sentence (once as a verb and once in the noun denoting the meal). Thus, "Ich esse das Mittagessen/Abendessen." in which "essen" appears twice, is incorrect. Instead, substitute the noun with "zu Mittag/Abend": "Ich esse zu Mittag." If "essen" is not used, then the complete noun is used: "Was gibt es zum Abendessen?" "Wir gehen in die Mensa zum Mittagessen."

24. (A)

When requesting identification, a name, the only syntactic form can be "Wie heißt...?" "Was heißt" means "was bedeutet", (i.e., what does (something) mean?) In other words, "was heißt" is a request for a definition or a translation.

25. (D)

"Ilse and Ingrid had to work yesterday." The imperfective forms of all modal auxiliaries contain the "te", "test", "te", etc. endings and have no umlauts."Mussen" does not exist. "Müssen" is present tense and makes no sense with "gestern" (past tense)."Müßten" is a subjunctive form.

26. (A)

"Wie" is used in comparisons before nouns ("so groß wie ein Elefant") and before pronouns and adjectives ("so reich wie er; so bald wie möglich") -- the "so ... wie" pairing. But is is not used before clauses. Thus "sobald" is used (spelled as one word).

27. (B)

"Studieren" does not mean "to study" in the sense of "to do one's homework", "to prepare a lesson", "to study for a test or quiz", etc., a fact that is unfortunately not clearly stated (or simply incorrectly stated) in many textbooks. "Lernen" is appropriate for use in kindergarten to 12th grade. "Hausaufgaben machen/schreiben" would probably be more commonly used by German Gymnasiasten (middle- and high school students). German university students, on the other hand, would be more likely to use "arbeiten", "lesen", "mich vorbereiten", or some other similar expression. "Studieren" is used in the sense of attending a university, being a university student (e.g., "Sie studiert vier Semester in Freiburg."), learning an academic discipline (e.g., "Er studiert Jura."), or --by extension-- investigating or analyzing something (e.g., "Wir wollen dieses Problem eingehend studieren.").

28. (C)

The subjunctive is often used in indirect discourse, especially in cautious reporting (where there is some question as to the truth or accuracy of the statement by a second party) or in formal noncommittal reporting. In indirect discourse and in questions, the special subjunctive (subjunctive I) can be used if its form is not identical with the indicative verb forms. If it is the same, the general subjunctive (subjunctive II) should be used. Subjunctive I is formed by adding the suffixes -e, -est, -e, -en, -et, and -en to the verb's infinitive stem; e.g., spreche, sprechest, spreche, etc. And arbeite, arbeitest, arbeite, etc.

29. (A)

For a discussion of the use of subjunctive in indirect discourse, see test item number 28, above. In that item, the forms of indirect discourse for present and future time situations were explained. Here we have a past time situation. In past time situations (past subjunctive), use a subjunctive I or II form (sei/wär) for verbs requiring "sein" to form the perfect tense, or a subjunctive I or II form of "haben" ("er habe/hätte", etc.) and the past participle of the main verb. Thus, "Er sei dahingefahren", since "fahren" requires "sein" here, is the correct answer.

30. (C)

"Kennen" is like "denken," "brennen," and others called "mixed" verbs or "irregular weak verbs" whose stem vowels, when the verb is in its imperfect form, change from "e" to "a" before the normal imperfect suffixes are attached: "ich kannte," "du dachtest," "es brannte," "rennen, senden, " etc. Thus, Inge never knew her benefactor, Mr. Smith: "...kannte Inge den Herrn Schmidt nie." "Konnte" (the imperfect form of "kann") and "könnte" (the present subjunctive form of "kann") are incorrect choices because, as modal verbs, they require an infinitive. "Kennte" does not exist in German.

31. (A)

Remember, for the "three c's" (<u>c</u>ity, <u>c</u>ountry, <u>c</u>ontinent) one most often will need "nach" to mean "to." Sometimes, if the country requires the definite article with it, and there are very few of these, one might use "in" to mean "to": "Er fährt morgen in die Schweiz."

32. (D)

The present participle is most widely used as a modifying adjective, and it is formed as follows: verb infinitive + <u>d</u> (+ adjective ending). It is translated most often in English as verb + "ing": singen + <u>d</u> + en = singenden = singing: "The singing children sound nice." Likewise: fliegen + <u>d</u> + e (adj. end.) = der <u>fliegende</u> Adler (the flying eagle): "Die <u>suchende</u> Mutter fand das <u>weinende</u> Kind," (the searching mother found the crying child).

33. (D)

Weak masculine nouns, also called "n-nouns," usually designate a male's station in life (profession, livelihood, activity, pastime), and they will have "(e)n" endings in the oblique cases (accusative, dative, and genitive cases). Such nouns usually end in "-t" (Student, Tourist, Polizist), in "-ph" (Philosoph, Geograph), and in "-nom" (Astronom). "Herr," "Junge," "Mensch" are also weak masculine nouns.

Thus, "Dem Piloten" (dative; indirect object), "des Studenten" (genetive; possession) are the correct answers.

34. (C)

"When Hans was in New York, he was afraid to use the subway."

Infinitive constructions in German consist of "zu" and the infinitive. The use of "nach" is incorrect according to this definition. "Fressen" means "to eat," and is used when referring to an animal that is eating. Technically, choice (A) is grammatically correct, but it would make sense only under very specific conditions.

35. (A)

The dative reflexive pronouns (mir, dir, sich/uns, euch, sich) are frequently used when more than just minimal interest is involved (and so is called the "dative of interest"). The dative of interest is optional and occurs with verbs such as "kaufen," "holen," "bestellen," etc. This dative reflexive pronoun is used only if there is a direct object in the sentence ("Programm" in this sentence).

36. (C)

An unreal (contrary-to-fact) condition in past time is expressed by a conditional clause (the "wenn" clause) whose verb is in its past subjunctive form; the past subjunctive form of a verb consists of the subjunctive form of "haben" or "sein" and the past participle of the verb itself. In the sentence, both "hätte gesagt" (had he said) and "wären abgefahren" (we would have gone) are in the past subjunctive.

37. (B)

An unreal (contrary-to-fact) condition in past time also includes the conclusion ("dann/so" clause) expressed in the past subjunctive:

...dann/so wären wir länger geblieben.
...then we would have stayed longer.
(Also: ...dann/so hätten wir mit Peter gesprochen.
...then we would have spoken with Peter.)

38. (A)

"Denn," like all the other coordinating conjunctions, is followed by a phrase that has regular word order (subject – verb) (choice A), not inverted word order (verb – subject) (choice B), and not transposed word order (verb is last, as with subordinating conjunctions (choice C)). Choice (D) is not correct because the subject of the second clause is missing.

39. (C)

If this person is doing laundry, chauferring children around, cleaning, and other obligations and does this at all hours, yet does not see monetary reimbursement for all this work; she must be a homemaker.

40. (D)

Such a hard-working person is not wasteful, lazy, flighty, absent-minded, or anything else. She can only be hard-working and industrious to accomplish all these chores.

41. (A)

She is not well-paid, poorly paid, or otherwise; she is simply not paid at all. There is no remuneration for her work.

42. (C)

Most of her work is accomplished at home. That is why she is known as a homemaker (Hausfrau).

43. (D)

It is the family members who are not especially grateful or who usually do not show their thanks often enough for her untiring work.

44. (B)

These family members too frequently take the homemaker's work for granted, work that they expect to be done without their necessarily deserving it or having earned it.

45. (D)

It is not the house, and most people do not own and work in their own park. Grass is only part of what is being described. But it also includes a playing area with a "Schaukel," an eating area with a "Tisch," a resting area with a "Stuhl," and a garden ("Beete gießen"). So it must be a family's "Garten," which we understand as a "yard," and not strictly as a "garden," which would be more specifically labelled as "Blumengarten, "Gemüsegarten," "Obstgarten," etc., to differentiate it from "Garten" in general: the backyard.

46. (C)

The only thing that could be multicolored, colorful, many-colored ("bunt") is the flowers. The "Schnee" and "Rasen" are each one color (white and green, respectively), and this designation for father is ridiculous.

47. (C)

A "Spatz" (also "Sperling") is a sparrow. Do not confuse the word with "Spaten" (spade), a garden utensil (Gartengerät).

48. (B)

Father would relax from his work done at his job (livelihood) or done in this backyard. We doubt he would rest up from his vacation because one goes on vacation in order to relax. Likewise, one takes a nap to rest and not to relax from afterwards.

49. (A)

If it is giving us pleasure ("Freude"), then it is giving us enjoyment ("Spaß"), and not worries ("Kummer," "Sorgen") or a lot of work ("Arbeit").

50. (D)

One doubts a person would take such pains to bury a doll or teddy bear; they would not be designated with an age ("von knapp 8 Jahren"). It is not a "Mann," since this being passed away "im Alter von knapp 8 Jahren." It must be a pet.

51. (C)

The pet died. Clues: "für immer friedlich eingeschlafen," "er hinter läßt," "sur letzten Ruhe gebettet," "Gott ... Deine ... Seele ... aufnehmen."

52. (A)

The pet lived with two people: "Er hinter läßt zwei traurige Herzen ... ." The "Freunde" are people who knew the pet but surely did not live as part of the family with the pet.

53. (B)

Obviously, they are unhappy that the pet died ("traurige Herzen"). They are not happy, untroubled, or furious.

54. (C)

The pet is referred to as "er," "ihn," and "lieber." Thus, it is not a "Katze" ("sie; liebe"). It is not a horse because it is a "kleine Seele," making this a small animal and not one as large as a horse. Dragons are mythical, not actual beasts.

55. (D)

"Wir haben ihn zur letzten Ruhe gebettet." Hence, he was buried. He was not forgotten, stuffed, or thrown away.

56. (A)

Limiting numerical adjectives, such as "einige," "wenige," "mehrere," "viele" are treated as unpreceded adjectives, i.e., the attributive (modifying) adjectives following them take the same (strong) endings, except in the genitive case; nominative and accusative: einige gute Freunde; dative: einigen guten Freunden; genetive: einiger guten Freunde.

57. (B)

"Von" requires objects in the dative case, so the dative personal pronoun "Ihnen" is required here; "dir" cannot be used because the person is being addressed as "Sie" ("Wissen Sie"), a formal form, so that formal form must be used again ("Ihnen" -- formal, not "dir" -- the informal, familiar form).

58. (A)

The relative pronoun "die" refers to the "Freunde": Ich habe die [Freunde] besucht. Thus, the relative pronoun is the object of the verb "besuchen." Since direct objects are in the accusative case, we need here the accusative plural relative pronoun, which is "die."

59. (C)

The names of a few countries are always preceded by some form of the definite article, and they all happen to be feminine: die Schweiz, die Türkei, die Tschechoslowakei, and a few others. So only the last two options are possible here. Since the friends "drove to Switzerland" -- motion toward an object (wohin?) -- we use the "accusative of motion toward," which, for the feminine singular, is "die."

60. (A)

"They rendered Paula this honor three times," In this phrase, "sie" is the subject and is therefore in the nominative case, "Paula" is the indirect object, and is therefore in the dative case (although it can only be understood as dative in context; "Paula" has no articles), and "Ehre" must therefore be in the accusative case; "Ehre" is feminine, so the correct adjective is "diese."

61. (B)

The honor was paid to me; therefore, "me" is the indirect object. Since the indirect object is in the dative case, the dative pronoun "mir" is needed here.

62. (B)

The comparative form of "oft" (often) is "öfter" (more often) and the superlative form is "am öftesten" (most often), not "öfters," which means "frequently," and is not used very much except in more informal usage: "Sie sprachen öfters von ihm." "They talked frequently about him." "They mentioned him frequently."

63. (A)

"She received the honor more often than I." In both languages, the nominative form of "I" is correct; e.g., "Er ist größer als ich/du." -- He is taller than I/you. In German, as in English, the case of the first noun in a comparison ("sie", which is nominative) determines the cases of any other nouns in that comparison ("ich", which is also nominative).

64. (D)

Usually when you have a verb that is used with "über," then the noun following "über" is in the accusative case: "Du schreibst/klagst (etc.). über das Wetter/den Mann, (etc.)." "Über," in this sentence, means "above," and in such instances, always takes objects that are in their accusative forms.

65. (C)

"Was" must be used as the relative pronoun for all indefinite pronoun antecedents or when referring to an entire clause (idea). Thus "was" follows "alles," "nichts," "vieles," "etwas," etc., because these are indefinite pronouns.

66. (C)

If the relative pronoun must answer the question "where?" (wo?), use the dative case (unless a preposition that takes a noun in the accusative or genitive case is used); therefore "dem" (for the singular, dative masculine "Brief"), is the proper article.

67. (A)

A da(r)-compound refers only to things or ideas, and not to a person. When referring back to a person, use the preposition and a pronoun, as here: "von ihm."

68. (B)

Adjectives following "ein" -words have mixed (neither weak nor strong) declensions; i.e., they have the endings -e, -es, -er, or -en, depending on case, gender, and number. Here "Student" is masculine, nominative, and singular, so the adjective "nett" has an "-er" suffix: "netter."

69. (D)

Indefinite times, expressed as "one" or "some" in English (one day/year, some day/year, etc.) are expressed by the "genitive of indefinite time." Therefore, "one day" becomes "eines Tages" (genitive form), and not "ein Tag" (nominative form).

70. (A)

Nationalities, religions, and professions usually do not include the indefinite article ("Er ist Amerikaner/Katholik/Arzt") unless an adjective is included: "Er ist ein junger Amerikaner."

71. (C)

"Menschen" is in the dative, plural case since "helfen" is a verb requiring the dative case. The adjective "ander__" is declined as strong since it has no "der"–word (weak declension) or "ein"–word (mixed declension) preceding it. Therefore, the proper suffix for the "ander–" root is "–en."

72. (B)

Not the animals' temperament, size, or general appearance is discussed, but their weapons and types of protection are given here (teeth, horns, speed, etc.).

73. (D)

The rabbit's best defense is its speed.

74. (C)

Three animals are mentioned that have horns (Stier, Nashorn, Büffel); the "Elefant" has tusks "Stoßzähne."

75. (D)

Obviously, these people are pretty stupid. When the writer calls them "intelligent," he is purposely being rather sarcastic.

76. (A)

Schilda is the name of an imaginary village ("im Dorfe Schilda" -- "in the village of Schilda"). It is not a country or any kind of city.

77. (B)

In the third sentence, "...und auf der anderen Seite des Berges trugen sie sie wieder hinunter," the second "sie" refers to the logs: "...and on the other side of the mountain/hill, they carried them [the logs] down again." The first "sie" refers to the Schildbürger, to the citizens of Schilda, of course.

78. (C)

Two examples of the citizens' stupidity are given here: First, we see how stupidly they carry the logs back up the mountain again just so they can roll them down; second, we see that their solution to getting light into the building is to permanently remove the roof, rather than to have built windows in the first place!

79. (D)

The logs for the Rathaus (city hall) come from trees in the nearby forest, not from a concrete factory or from anywhere else. We can assume the citizens chop down the trees in the nearby forest to obtain the logs for their building.

80. (C)

Since the citizens had no light in their completed building, and they got no light until they removed the roof, we know they forgot to add windows in their original building plans. (It is even stated in the passage – – read carefully!)

GERMAN TEST IV

PART A

Time: 1 Hour
80 Questions

DIRECTIONS: Each of the sentences in this part has a blank space indicating that a word of phrase has been omitted. From the four choices select the ONE that, when inserted in the sentence, fits grammatically and logically with the sentence as a whole. Then blacken the corresponding space on the answer sheet.

1. Wann _________ du geboren?

   (A) warst

   (B) wurdest

   (C) bist

   (D) wirst

2. ________ Mann war mein Freund.

   (A) Diese

   (B) Dieser

   (C) Diesen

   (D) Dieses

3. Welche Vorlesungen ________ du?

   (A) besuchst

   (B) versuchst

(C) behandelst

(D) nimmst

4. Er setzte sich neben ________.

(A) die Dame

(B) der Dame

(C) einer Dame

(D) einem Dame

5. Was nimmst du? ________ du eine Cola?

(A) Möchtest

(B) Mag

(C) Mögt

(D) Mögen

6. Es ist schwer, _____ 6 uhr aufzustehen.

(A) zu

(B) am

(C) um

(D) an

7. Er macht ________ Sorgen, daß sie nicht kommt.

(A) ihn

(B) sich

(C) ihm

(D) sein

8. Was fehlt ________?

(A) dir

(B) dein

(C) dich

(D) sich

9. Er ist ________ als ich.

(A) größere

(B) größer

(C) großer

(D) größt

10. Das ________ weh!

(A) macht

(B) tun

(C) tut

(D) ist

11. Das ist die Dame, ________ Handtasche ich fand.

(A) dessen

(B) der

(C) deren

(D) wessen

12. Das war Liebe auf den ersten ________!

(A) Schlag

(B) Blick

(C) Aussicht

(D) Blickwinkel

13. ______________ Mann hast du gesehen?

(A) Welch für einen

(B) Welch für ein

(C) Was für einen

(D) Welche für ein

14. Was du sagst, ist ________ egal.

(A) mir

(B) ihr

(C) dich

(D) mich

15. Er glaubt, daß er immer _________.

(A) recht ist

(B) recht hat

(C) richtig hat

(D) Rechnung hat

16. Nimmst du ________ teil?

(A) davor

(B) da an

(C) daran

(D) darüber

17. Er ist stolz ________ seine Kinder.

(A) an

(B) vor

(C) über

(D) auf

18. Trinken Sie ________ Milch oder Tee?

(A) liebst

(B) gerner

(C) lieber

(D) lieb

19. Wo hast du das Buch ________?

(A) gekommen

(B) bekommt

(C) gekommt

(D) bekommen

20. Sie ________ immer gut ________.

(A) sieht . . . an

(B) sieht . . . aus

(C) sieht . . . um

(D) sieht . . . über

21. Karl __________ gestern von einem Hund angefallen.

(A) werde

(B) wär

(C) wurde

(D) wären

22. Das höre ich ________ in meinem Leben!

(A) zum erstenmal

(B) für das erste Mal

(C) vorerst

(D) zuerst

23. Er hat ________ Mai Geburtstag.

(A) in

(B) zu

(C) am

(D) im

24. Mit Welchem Zug ________ er ________?

(A) kommt...um

(B) kommt...vor

(C) kommt...mit

(D) kommt...an

25. Hans ist ________.

(A) Student

(B) ein Student

(C) einen Studenten

(D) ein Studenten

26. Ich komme direkt von ________.

(A) zu Hause

(B) Hause

(C) nach Hause

(D) Haus

27. ______________ soll man das nicht machen.

(A) In meiner Meinung

(B) Nach meiner Meinung

(C) Meine Meinung

(D) Meiner Meinung nach

28. Wenn ich will, kann ich Pilot ________.

(A) werden

(B) bekommen

(C) werde

(D) bekomme

29. ________ kalt.

(A) Ich bin

(B) Mich ist

(C) Zu mir ist es

(D) Mir ist

30. ________ Buch ist das?

(A) Wessen

(B) Wer

(C) Wem

(D) Wen

31. Er Kommt ________ vorbei.

(A) heute abend

(B) heute nacht

(C) gestern abend

(D) gestern nacht

32. Er ________, wie ich heiße.

(A) kennt

(B) weiß

(C) weißt

(D) kannte

33. ________ Kind kann brav sein.

(A) Jeder

(B) Jeden

(C) Jede

(D) Jedes

34. Er ________ die Haare schneiden.

(A) ver läßt sich

(B) läßt sich

(C) ver läßt

(D) läßt

35. Das Buch gehört________ nicht.

(A) ihr

(B) sie

(C) ihn

(D) dich

36. ________ Koffer hast du?

(A) Welcher

(B) Welchen

(C) Welches

(D) Welche

37. Sie möchte nach Deutschland ________.

(A) führen

(B) gefahren

(C) zu fahren

(D) fahren

38. ________ Brötchen sind schwer zu finden.

(A) Gutes

(B) Guten

(C) Gute

(D) Gut

PART B

DIRECTIONS: Read the following passages carefully for comprehension. Each passage is followed by a number of incomplete statements or questions. Select the completion or answer that is best according to the passage and blacken the corresponding space on the answer sheet.

Eines Tages wollten eine Mutter und ihre Tochter, wie sie es gewohnt waren, zusammen in die Stadt fahren, um Einkaufe zu machen. Diesmal war die Mutter an der Reihe, die Tochter abzuholen. Als sie aus der Einfahrt fuhren, sah die Mutter den alten, treuen Familienhund, der vor dem Haus schlief. Nach einigen Stunden in der Stadt machten die Frauen sich auf dem Rückweg. [Unterwegs trafen sie plötzlich auf einen toten Hund in der Straße, der von einem Auto übergefahren worden war.] Die Mutter erkannte ihn sofort und fragte die Tochter erschrocken, ob das nicht ihr Hund sei. Die Tochter traute sich nicht, aus dem Auto auszusteigen, um den Hund genauer anzusehen. Endlich machte die Mutter es und kam mit der traurigen Nachricht zuruck, das sei tatsächlich ihr lieber "Waldi". Als die zwei Damen ratlos da standen und fast hysterisch weinten, kam ein Mann vorbei und fragte, ob er ihnen irgendwie behilflich sein könnte. Die Mutter, die sich einigermaßen gefasst hatte, bat ihn, den Hund in den Kofferraum zu legen, damit sie ihn nach Hause bringen und begraben könnten. Das machte er und die beiden fuhren dann tränenerstickt nach Hause. Unterwegs überlegten sie, wie sie es den Kindern sagen würden usw. Als sie in die Einfahrt fuhren, fing die Mutter an, laut zu lachen: Dort vor dem Haus schlief immer noch der alte, treue Familienhund! Wem gehörte der fremde Hund im Kofferraum??!

39. Die Mutter und die Tochter...

(A) haben in der Stadt gewohnt.

(B) fuhren selten zusammen in die Stadt.

(C) wollten zusammen in der Stadt wohnen.

(D) wollten zusammen einkaufen gehen.

40. Die Mutter...

(A) wurde von der Tochter abgeholt.

(B) holte die Tochter ab, weil das ihre Gewohnheit war.

(C) holte manchmal die Tochter ab.

(D) holte immer die Tochter ab.

41. Auf dem Rückweg...

(A) haben sie einen Hund in der Straße überfahren.

(B) haben sie einen überfahrenen Hund in der Straße gesehen.

(C) haben sie einen toten Hund überfahren.

(D) haben sie einen überfahrenen, aber noch nicht toten Hund gesehen (in der Straße gesehen).

42. Der Mann...

(A) legte den überfahrenen Hund in den Kofferraum.

(B) fragte, ob er ihr Hund sei.

(C) hat aus Versehen den Hund überfahren.

(D) wollte den Hund begraben.

43. Als sie den toten Hund fanden...

(A) weinten sie vor Freude.

(B) wurden sie fast hysterisch.

(C) glaubten sie "Waldi" sei noch zu Hause.

(D) wollten sie ihn dort lassen.

44. "Waldi"...

(A) mußte begraben werden.

(B) wurde vom Mann im Garten begraben.

(C) freute sich als die Frauen ankamen.

(D) schlief noch vor dem Haus.

Eine Amerikanerin, deren Deutsch nicht einwandfrei war, studierte an der Universität von Heidelberg. Wie viele von ihren Kommilitonen, ist sie im Laufe des Jahres in finanzielle Schwierigkeiten geraten. Sie war verzweifelt. Die Eltern waren weit weg; eine Stelle zu finden kam wegen der Schwierigkeiten eines Ausländers, eine Arbeitsgenehmigung zu bekommen nicht in Frage; und Geld von den genauso armen Freunden zu borgen war unmöglich. Nach langen Zögern und langer Überlegung entschloß sie sich, Blut zu spenden - eine Lösung, die nicht selten auch von deutschen Studenten gefunden wird. Also eines Tages nahm sie sich zusammen und suchte die Stelle auf, wo man Blut spenden kann. Der junge, gutaussehende Krankenpfleger, der hinter einem großen Schreibtisch saß, schien sehr freundlich zu sein. Die Freunde der Studentin hatten ihr genau beigebracht, wie sie sich ausdrücken sollte. Zu ihrer großen Erleichterung verstand er alles, was sie sagte, aber als er sie ansprach, hörte sie nur deutlich das eine Wort "ziehen." Schon in dem ersten Deutschkurs in Amerika hat sie Obwohl es ihr etwas extrem schien, sich auszuziehen, um Blut zu lassen, zögerte sie nicht lange, weil sie Geld brauchte. Der Krankenpfleger war beschäftig und arbeitete weiter am Schreibtisch, ohne sich um sie zu kümmern. Die Amerikanerin zog sich aus und nörte nicht auf, bis sie splitternackt vor ihm stand. Als der Krankenpfleger hochschaute, sah sie wie er sich zu beherrschen versuchte und gegen Gelächter kämpfte. Mit großer Anstrengung ist es ihm gelungen, genügend Herr über sich zu werden, um ganz langsam and deutlich sagen zu können: "Sie hätten nur den Ärmel hochziehen müssen!"

45. Die Amerikanerin wollte Blut spenden, weil...

(A) sie Geld brauchte.

(B) sie weit weg von ihren Eltern war.

(C) sie eine Stelle suchte.

(D) ihre Freunde ihr nicht helfen wollten.

46. Sie konnte keine Stelle suchen, weil...

(A) ihre Eltern dagegen waren.

(B) ihre Freunde nicht arbeiteten.

(C) Ausländer ohne Erlaubnis nicht arbeiten dürfen.

(D) sie Geld von ihren Freunden borgen könnte.

47. Die Studentin...

(A) verstand alles, was der Krankenpfleger sagte.

(B) verstand nur ein Teil davon, was der Krankenpfleger sagte.

(C) verstand nichts davon, was der Krankenpfleger sagte.

(D) verstand genau, was der Krankenpfleger sagte.

48. Der Krankenpfleger kümmerte sich nicht um sie, weil...

(A) er wußte, daß sie Geld brauchte.

(B) er mit seiner Arbeit beschäftigt war.

(C) er sich zu beherrschen versuchte.

(D) er lachte.

49. Die Studentin zog sich aus, weil...

(A) der Arzt es ihr befahl.

(B) sie nicht zögern wollte.

(C) sie falsch verstanden hatte.

(D) der Arzt es langsam und deutlich sagte.

Die Schauspieler des Deutschen Schauspielhauses in Hamburg suchen einen ihrer Hauptdarsteller--den Hundestar "Aaron". Aaron ist ein Mischlingshund, der in Shakespeares "Wie es Euch gefällt" die Rolle eines Hirtenhundes spielt. Als er zum letzten Mal gesehen wurde, war er auf Urlaub in Bayern, wo er einen Spaziergang durch den Wald machte. Seitdem wartet nicht nur sein Besitzer, der den Schäfer in der klassischen Komödie spielt, sondern das gesamte Ensemble auf ein Lebenszeichen von ihm. Sie seien alle ganz verzweifelt und traurig, sagte eine Sprecherin des Schauspielhauses. Warum ist Aaron weggelaufen? Er ist wieder ein Opfer seiner Leidenschaften geworden.

Er hat sich nämlich in eine Hündin namens "Sissy" verliebt. Seit dieser Liebe auf dem ersten Blick ist das Paar verschwunden. Der mittelgroße, blonde Aaron hatte immer eine Vorliebe für große langbeinige Hundedamen. Das Ensemble will nicht die kleinste Chance auslassen, den Star wiederzubekommen. Sie wissen jedoch nicht, wie es weitergehen soll.

50. Wen suchen die Schauspieler des Deutschen Schauspielhauses?

(A) Einen weggelaufenen Hund

(B) Einen Mann, der einer ihrer Haupdarsteller ist

(C) Einen Hirtenhund, der die Rolle von Aaron spielt

(D) Einen Hund, der eine Rolle in einem Stück von Shakespeare spielen könnte

51. Wie ist der Hund verlorengegangen?

(A) Auf einer Reise nach Bayern hat er sich verfahren.

(B) Während eines Spazierganges ist er verschwunden.

(C) Er wollte allein durch den Wald laufen.

(D) Er wollte Urlaub in Bayern machen.

52. Er ist weggelaufen, weil...

(A) er nicht mehr arbeiten wollte.

(B) er sich verliebt hat.

(C) er verschwinden wollte.

(D) er weitergehen wollte.

53. Wer wartet auf sein Rückkehr?

(A) Nur sein Besitzer interessiert sich dafür.

(B) Nur eine Sprecherin des Schauspielhauses ist daran interessiert.

(C) Nur ein Schäfer macht sich Sorgen.

(D) Nicht nur sein Besitzer, sondern auch die Schauspieler hoffen, daß er wiederkommt.

54. Aaron und Sissy sind vielleicht ein komisches Paar, weil...

(A) Aaron Schauspieler ist.

(B) Sissy keine Schauspielerin ist.

(C) Aaron zu leidenschaftlicht ist.

(D) sie anders aussehen.

PART C

DIRECTIONS: The sentences below contain blank spaces indicating omissions in the text. Below each blank are four choices. Select the choice that is grammatically correct in the context and blacken the corresponding space on the answer sheet. Be sure to read the sentences first.

Ich __________nicht__________er kommt, aber wir

55. (A) weißte
    (B) wußte
    (C) wüßte
    (D) gewußt

56. (A) woher
    (B) wo
    (C) wohin
    (D) wozu

__________, daß wir aus dem__________Stadtteil von

57. (A) stellten fest
    (B) feststellten
    (C) haben gefeststellt
    (D) wurden festgestellt

58. (A) gleichen
    (B) gleiche
    (C) gleiches
    (D) gleich

Berlin stammen.

Gestern ______________in _______ Bibliothek

59. (A) ein Fremder hat mich
(B) hat ein Fremder mich
(C) mich ein Fremder hat
(D) mich hat ein Fremder

60. (A) der
(B) die
(C) dem
(D) den

angesprochen. Er wollte wissen, _______ich je etwas von Hesse

61. (A) wenn
(B) obwohl
(C) wen
(D) ob

______________.

62. (A) lessen wollen habe
(B) lesen wollen hat
(C) hat lesen wollen
(D) habe lesen wollen

An deiner Stelle ____________ ich ____________ gesagt,

63. (A) wäre
(B) hatte
(C) hätte
(D) hat

64. (A) er
(B) ihn
(C) ihm
(D) es

er ______________ morgen ______________.

65. (A) müsse
(B) müßt
(C) müssen
(D) mußt

66. (A) kommen wieder
(B) wiederzukommen
(C) zu wiederkommen
(D) wiederkommen

______________________________, ______________ ich Lust,

67. (A) Nachdem war ich in Berlin
(B) Nachdem in Berlin ich war
(C) Nachdem ich war in Berlin
(D) Nachdem ich in Berlin war

68. (A) habe
(B) hatte
(C) hätte
(D) habte

__________ Köln zu fahren.

69. (A) nach
(B) in
(C) zu
(D) bei

Das Fenster __________ jeden Tag ________________, sonst

70. (A) wird ...zugemacht
(B) ist ... zugemacht
(C) würde ... zugemacht
(D) wurde ... zumachen

____________________ alles ____________________.

71. (A) war ... kaputtgegangen
(B) ware ... kaputtgegangen
(C) ist ... kaputtgegangen
(D) würde ... kaputtgehen

PART D

DIRECTIONS: Read the following passages carefully for comprehension. Each passage is followed by a number of incomplete statements or questions. Select the completion or answer that is best according to the passage and blacken the corresponding space on the answer sheet.

Zwei junge Leute haben eine Nacht im Königspalast in Amsterdam verbracht. Gegen ein oder zwei Uhr stiegen sie über ein Baugerüst auf dem Dach des Palasts. Das hatten sie schon einmal getan, aber jetzt wollten sie ins Innere des Palasts gehen. Das gelang ihnen ohne Schwierigkeiten durch ein Dachfenster. In der königlichen Küche verzehrten sie chinesische Delikatessen. Nacher nahmen sie ungestört ein Bad und schliefen selig in einem Luxusbett ein. Alles wäre wahrscheinlich gut gegangen, wenn die beiden ehemaligen Studenten an der Kunstakademie nicht zehn Bilder als Andenken an ihr nächtliches Abenteuer nicht hätte mitnehmen wollen. Ein Hausdiener erwischte die beiden und übergab sie der Polizei. Wegen des Diebbstahls mußten beide eine Strafe bezahlen. Die Übernachtung im Palast kam sie fast doppelt so teuer zu stehen wie eine Übernachtung im teuersten Hotel der Stadt.

72. Wie ist es dem jungen Paar gelungen, in den Palast zu kommen?

(A) Sie gingen ohne Mühe durch ein Fenster im Dach.

(B) Sie gingen durch die königliche Küche.

(C) Sie stiegen über ein Baugerüst und fanden eine Tür.

(D) Sie schauten durch ein Dachfenster und warteten bis niemand in der Küche war.

73. Nachdem sie im Palast waren,

(A) hatten sie viel Angst.

(B) trauten sie sich nicht, etwas zu essen.

(C) fühlten sie sich, als ob sie zu Hause wären.

(D) wollten sie gleich wieder gehen.

74. Warum wurden sie erwischt?

(A) Weil sie ein Bad nehmen wollten.

(B) Weil sie essen wollten.

(C) Weil sie schlafen wollten.

(D) Weil sie sich für die Kunst interessierten.

75. Die Übernachtung...

(A) war teuer, weil sie eine Strafe bezahlen mußten.

(B) war fast so teuer wie in einem Hotel.

(C) war billiger als in einem teueren Hotel.

(D) war so teuer wie im teuersten Hotel der Stadt.

In Deutschland gibt es ein reichliches Angebot an Ausflugsmöglichkeiten, die von Firmen veranstaltet werden, um ihre Produkte zu verkaufen. Es gibt zweierlei solcher Fahrten: Butterfahrten und Kaffeefahrten. Butterfahrten sind immer mit einer Seefahrt verbunden und nennen sich Butterfahrten, weil man auf dem Schiff Butter und andere Produkte zu einem günstigen Werbungen für diese Fahrten. Eine typische Reklame lautet so: "Wir fahren mit dem Luxusreisebus durch das herrliche Schleswig-Holstein in die idyllische Hafenstadt Heiligenhafen. Unterwegs haben Sie die Möglichkeit an einer informativen Verkaufsveranstaltung teilzunehmen. Anschließend machen wir eine Ostsee-Kreuzfahrt. Zollfreier Einkauf an Bord von Zigaretten, Spirituosen, Kaffee, u.s.w." Diese Butterfahrt kostet nur DM 24.90 (ungefähr $14). Im Preis enthalten sind die Busfahrt, ein Mittagessen, die Ostsee-Fahrt, und einige Werbegeschenke, wie Brot, Eier, Schinken, Honig und Wurst. Kaffefahrten unterscheiden sich von Butterfahrten dadurch, daß keine Seefahrt dabei ist. Sie nennen sich Kaffeefahrten, weil die Teilnehmer unterwegs ins Cafe gehen und Kaffee trinken. Eine typische Kaffeefahrt besteht aus einer Reise im Reisebus, einer Übernachtung mit Frühstück und einer Dampferfahrt am Rhein mit einer Reiseleitung. Sie kostet nur DM 69. Alle Unkosten sind im Preis enthalten. Von den Teilnehmern an Kaffee- und Butterfahrten wird es erwartet, daß sie irgendwo unterwegs an einer "informativen Verkaufsveranstaltung" teilnehmen. Das bedeutet, daß teuere Produkte vorgeführt werden, in der Hoffnung, daß die Teilnehmer möglichst viel Geld ausgeben werden. Wenn man jedoch der Versuchung, etwas zu kaufen widerstehen kann, kann man einen schönen Ausflug für wenig Geld genießen.

76. Die Veranstalter von Butter-und Kaffeefahrten wollen…

(A) Produkte verkaufen.

(B) Ausflüge zu billigen Preisen anbieten.

(C) den Teilnehmern ein Vergnügen bereiten.

(D) Butter und Kaffee verkaufen.

77. Wie unterscheiden sich Butter-und Kaffeefahrten?

(A) Auf einer Butterfahrt kauft man Butter und auf einer Kaffeefahrt kauft man Kaffe.

(B) Eine Butterfahrt bietet immer eine Seefahrt an.

(C) Auf einer Butterfahrt im Gegensatz zu einer Kaffeefahrt soll man vorgeführte Produkte kaufen.

(D) Eine Butterfahrt ist billiger als eine Kaffeefahrt.

78. Was ist ein Vorteil von Butter-und Kaffefahrten?

(A) Mann kann viel Butter und Kaffee kaufen.

(B) Man kann billige Ausflüge machen.

(C) Man kann immer zu günstigen Preisen Produkte kaufen.

(D) Man kann umsonst eine Reise machen.

79. Was ist ein Nachteil von Butter- und Kaffeefahrten?

(A) Die Reisen sind lang und ermüdend.

(B) Der kaffee schmeckt nicht.

(C) Die Butter ist teuer.

(D) Die vorgeführten Produkte sind teuer.

80. Was für Teilnehmer können von solchen Fahrten profitieren?

(A) Diejenigen, die wenig Geld haben aber doch die teueren Produkte kaufen wollen.

(B) Diejenigen, die viel Geld haben.

(C) Diejenigen, die der Versuchung Widerstehen können, die teueren Produkte zu kaufen.

(D) Diejenigen, die alles kaufen, was angeboten wird.

THE COLLEGE BOARD ACHIEVEMENT TEST IN GERMAN

TEST IV

ANSWER KEY

1.	C	21.	C	41.	B	61.	D
2.	B	22.	A	42.	A	62.	D
3.	A	23.	D	43.	B	63.	C
4.	A	24.	D	44.	D	64.	C
5.	A	25.	A	45.	A	65.	A
6.	C	26.	A	46.	C	66.	D
7.	B	27.	D	47.	B	67.	D
8.	A	28.	A	48.	B	68.	B
9.	B	29.	D	49.	C	69.	A
10.	C	30.	A	50.	A	70.	A
11.	C	31.	A	51.	B	71.	D
12.	B	32.	B	52.	B	72.	A
13.	C	33.	D	53.	D	73.	C
14.	A	34.	B	54.	D	74.	D
15.	B	35.	A	55.	B	75.	A
16.	C	36.	B	56.	A	76.	A
17.	D	37.	D	57.	A	77.	B
18.	C	38.	C	58.	A	78.	B
19.	D	39.	D	59.	B	79.	D
20.	B	40.	C	60.	A	80.	C

GERMAN TEST IV

DETAILED EXPLANATIONS OF ANSWERS

1. (C)

To state the birth date of a living person, the present tense of the verb "sein" is used. Answer (A) is incorrect, because it is in the imperfect tense. Choice (B) is the imperfect tense of the verb "werden." It would be correct if a deceased person's birth date were being discussed. One would ask, for example:

Wann wurde Beethoven geboren?

Choice (D) is the present tense of the verb "werden." It is used primarily to form the future tense and the passive. All of the answer choices are second person singular.

2. (B)

"Dieser" has the same endings as the definite article. If we were to substitute the definite article here, it would be "der". It is nominative masculine. Choice (A) would be correct if the subject were feminine (compare to "die"). Choice (C) is the accusative masculine form (compare to "den"). (D) is both nominative and accusative neuter (compare to "das/das").

3. (A)

"To attend" is often expressed in German by the verb "besuchen", which also means "to visit." Other examples:

Ich besuchte seine Schule. (I attended his school.)

Gestern abend besuchte ich ein Konzert. (Last night I attended a concert.)

Choice (B) is a form of the verb "versuchen" and means "to try". Choice (C) is derived from the verb "behandeln" and means "to treat". The last choice is derived from the verb "nehmen", which means "to take".

4. (A)

In order to do this, you need to know two things: The verb "sich setzen" is a verb of motion and "neben" is a two-way preposition. This means that its object is in the dative case, if no motion toward a goal is involved and in the accusative, if there is. Answer (A) is the only choice in the accusative case. Choices (B) and (C) are in the dative case and would be possible, if the verb were "sitzen". "Er sitzt neben der Dame" means "He is sitting next to the lady." "Er setzte sich neben die Dame" means "He seated himself next to the lady." Choice (D) would not be possible with "Dame", since "einem" is either a masculine or neuter form.

5. (A)

"Möchten" is one of the most common subjunctive forms in German and means "would like". Choices (B), (C), and (D) are also forms of the verb "mögen", but they are in the present tense. The present tense would be possible here, but none of them agree with the subject "du". (B) is the first and third person singular form. (C) is the second person plural form, and (D) is the infinitive.

6. (C)

In German, as in all languages, prepositions are difficult. Often they simply must be learned in context. The English "at" used before an expression of time is expressed by "um" in German. "Zu" in choice (A) generally means "to", but its meaning varies with the context. Choice (B) often means "at the". Choice (D), without the definite article (am= an dem) also can mean "at", but not in giving the time.

7. (B)

In order to answer this correctly, you must be familiar with the expression "sich Sorgen machen", which means "to be worried" in

English. Furthermore, you must know the reflexive pronoun for the third person singular subject "er". "Sich" is also the reflexive for third person plural. A quick review of reflexives:

ich: mich/mir	wir: uns
du: dich/dir	ihr: euch
er, sie, es: sich	sie: sich

Sie: sich

The reflexive forms of "ich" and "du" use the accusative reflexive (mich/dich) if there is no other accusative object:

Ich wasche mich.

The dative form is used, if there is:

Ich wasche mir die Hände.

Choice (A) is simply the accusative masculine pronoun. Choice (D) could either be the infinitive of the verb "to be" or the possessive adjective "his" or "its".

8. (A)

This is an idiom and one must know that the pronoun must be in the dative case. It means "What is wrong with you?" Choice (B) means "your" and doesn't fit, grammatically or logically. Choice (C) does not make sense, because it is in the wrong case. Choice (D) is a reflexive pronoun. It can't be used with a non-reflexive verb.

9. (B)

This is a comparative adjective and means "bigger". Choice (A) is correct as a comparative, but it has an adjectival ending and predicate adjectives (adjectives that do not come before nouns) do not have endings. Choice (C) is missing an umlaut. Most monosyllabic adjectives with the vowels a, o, or u have umlauts in their comparative forms. Choice (D) is a superlative form. However, it would have to be preceded either by the definite article (as in English: the biggest) and have an adjectival ending, or be preceded by "am".

10. (C)

This one is very simple, if you know the idiom "weh tun", which means "to hurt". Choice (A) uses the wrong verb. Although "tun" and "machen" can be interchanged, they are not so in this expression. Choice (B) is plural and does not agree with the singular subject. Like choice (A), choice (D) simply uses the wrong verb.

11. (C)

This is a relative pronoun. It means "whose". Whenever the meaning of a relative pronoun is "whose", it is in the genitive case, no matter how it is used in the relative clause. For example:

Das ist die Dame, in deren Tasche das Geld war.
That is the woman, in whose purse the money was.

In this sentence, "deren Tasche" is actually used as if it were dative. Choice (A) is masculine genitive and also means "whose." Answer (D) means "whose" in questions. For example:

Wassen Tasche ist das?
Whose purse is that?

A quick review of relative pronouns:

	MAS.	FEM.	N.	PL.
NOM.	der	die	das	die
ACC.	den	die	das	die
DAT.	dem	der	dem	denen
GEN.	dessen	deren	dessen	deren

Notice that they are like the definite article, except in the dative plural and all genitive forms, which are really just expanded versions of the definite article.

12. (B)

This corresponds to the English expression "love at first sight". Choice (A) might be possible, but would mean "love at first blow". Choice (C) means "view". Choice (D) means "view point".

13. (C)

The expression "was für ein" means "what kind of a". The case of "ein" depends upon how it is used in the sentence. In this example, it is the accusative object of the verb "sehen". Choices (A), (B), and (D) do not exist.

14. (A)

The idiom "egal sein" always takes a dative pronoun. This sentence means "What you say is all the same to me" or "I don't care what you say". Choices (B), (C), and (D) are all in the accusative case and therefore do not fit.

15. (B)

The idiom "recht haben" is equivalent to the English "to be right". Choice (A) is likely to sound right to an English-speaker, since we use the verb "to be" in this expression. Choice (C) does not exist. "Richtig" used alone means "correct" or "right". Choice (D) also does not exist. "Rechnung" means "bill" or "check". If we put in an article, the sentence would make sense:

Er hat die Rechnung.
He has the check/bill.

16. (C)

"Teilnehmen an" means "to participate in". The preposition "an" is used in a "da (r) construction". A "da(r) contruction" replaces a preposition and a pronoun referring to a thing. That is the case here: Are you participating IN IT? Choice (A) is also a "da(r) construction", but it has the wrong preposition. Choice (B) is incorrect, because there must be an "r" inserted when the preposition begins with a vowel. Choice (D) also has the wrong preposition.

17. (D)

The preposition used with "stolz" is "auf" and together, they means "proud of". There are many such unchangeable combinations of adjectives and prepositions that one must simply learn as they come up. The other prepositions cannot be used with "stolz".

18. (C)

"Gern" when used with a verb, means "to like" whatever the verb means. For example: Ich trinke gern Wein.
I like to drink wine.
Er singt gern.
He likes to sing.

"Gern" also has comparative and superlative forms, which are irregular. "Lieber" is the comparative and the superlative is "liebst-" used with "am" (adverb).

Examples: Ich trinke lieber Wein also Bier.
I prefer drinking wine to beer.
Ich trinke Bier gern, aber ich trinke Wein am liebsten.
I like drinking beer, but I prefer wine.

19. (D)

"Bekommen" means "to get" or "to receive". Its past participle, which is what is in this sentence, looks like the infinitive. Choice (A) is the past participle of the verb "kommen" (to come). Choice (B) is the third person singular present tense form of "bekommen":

Er bekommt das Buch von mir.
He is getting the book from me.

Choice (C) does not exist.

20. (B)

The verb "aussehen" means "to look", as in "to appear". The example says: She always looks good. Choice (A) means "to look at". An example of its use would be:

Sie sah mich komisch an.
She looked at me strangely.

Choice (C) means "to look around". However, it is reflexive and the reflexive particle is missing here. With the reflexive, the sentence would make sense: Sie sieht sich immer gut um.
She always has a good look around.

Choice (D), a form of "übersehen", means "to overlook", and does not fit.

21. (C)

This sentence uses the passive imperfect form of "anfallen" (to attack). Use of the passive voice indicates that the subject, Karl, is being acted upon. Whatever acts upon the subject (in this case, a dog) is usually preceded by "von", which always has a dative object (einem Hund). The passive form of a verb consists of the proper form of werden and the past participle of the verb itself (wurde angefallen). In this case, "gestern" indicates a past occurence, so choice (A), which is in the present tense, is incorrect. Choice (B) is incorrect because an action, not a state, is being described. Karl was not "in the state of being attacked". Choice (D) is not in the third person singular and would require the following of "angefallen" by "worden".

22. (A)

"For the first time" is expressed in German by "zum erstenmal". Choice (B) is a direct translation from English and does not exist. Choice (C) means "first of all", "for the present", or "for the time being". For example:

Ich möchte vorerst nichts machen.
For the time being, I would like to do nothing.

Choice (D) means "first". An example of its use:

Zuerst will ich etwas essen, dann schlafe ich.
First I want to eat something, then I will sleep.

23. (D)

Before months of the year, the preposition "in" and the definite article used in contracted form, "im". Since all months are masculine, "im" is always used. Choice (A) is lacking the definite article. Choice (B) could never be used in this context. Choice (C) would be correct, if the date were added:

Er hat am zweiten Mai Geburtstag.

24. (D)

"Ankommen" means "to arrive" and is the only logical choice here. Choice (A) might be possible, but it would be a bit drastic. "Umkommen" means "to die". Choice (B) means "to happen". A common German saying is:

Das kommt in den besten Familien vor.
That happens in the best of families. (In English, we would probably say, "That can happen to anyone.")

Choice (C) means "to come along" and does not fit grammatically.

25. (A)

Although it sounds strange to the ears of English-speakers, occupations and nationalities are not preceded by articles in German. For that reason, choices (B) and (C) are incorrect. Choice (C) is also in the wrong case. Choice (D) is also incorrect on two counts: It has an article, and the -en ending is only present in cases other than the nominative. Further examples of the omission of the article:

Er ist Hamburger.

He is a citizen of Hamburg. (if you put in the article, it would mean "He is a hamburger." Technically, John F. Kennedy's "Ich bin ein Berliner." means "I am a jelly donut.")

26. (A)

Although it might seem strange to have two prepositions together, it happens here. "Zu Hause" means "at home" and "home". This example means "He is coming directly from home."

"Hause" cannot be used alone, as in choice (B). Choice (C) means "(to) home" and would make no sense in this sentence. As with choice (B), "Haus" cannot stand alone here.

27. (D)

"In my opinion" is expressed with the phrase "meiner Meinung nach" in German. It is one of several such phrases in which the object of the preposition comes before the preposition. For this reason, choice (B) is not used. Choice (A) has the incorrect preposition. Choice (C) is incomplete.

28. (A)

Although the verb "werden" has several uses, here it means "to become". Choice (B) is a false cognate. It looks like the English "to become", but has a different meaning. It means "to get" or "to receive". Choice (C) is incorrect, because an infinitive is needed, and choice (C) is a conjugated form. Choice (D) is incorrect for the reasons given for (B) and (C).

29. (D)

This is an idiom that often confuses English speakers, since we simply say "I am cold." If one translates that literally into German, as in choice (A), the result is something quite different from what the speaker usually intends. It is closest to "I am frigid" in English. Choice (B) is impossible, because the sentence would have no subject, stated or understood. "Mich" can only be a direct object and the verb "sein" can never have a direct object. Choice (D) would be fine without the preposition "zu". It isn't necessary. When the blank is filled in correctly, "Mir ist kalt." It appears to be missing a subject. However, it is not uncommon to have the understood subject "es", and that is the case here.

30. (A)

All forms given here are interrogative forms. Only choice (A) fits. It means "whose". It is only used in questions. Choice (B) is the nominative form of "who". Choice (C) is the dative form. Choice (D) is the accusative form. Examples of their use are:

Wer ist das?
(Who is that?)
Wem gehört das?
(To whom does that belong?)
Wen sah er?
(Whom did he see?)

31. (A)

"Heute abend" corresponds to the English "this evening". Choice (B) has to do with bedtime. An example of its use is:

Ich hoffe, daß ich heute nacht besser schlafe.
(I hope that I will sleep better tonight.)

The same applies to choice (D). It has to do with bedtime and means "last night". Along the same line, one says "Guten Abend" as a greeting and "Gute Nacht" when going to bed. Choice (C) means "last night" and doesn't fit, because the verb is in the present tense.

32. (B)

There are two verbs in German meaning "to know". "Wissen" means "to know a fact". "Kennen" means "to be acquainted with" and has to do with knowing people and even books and places. The example has to do with knowing people and even books and places. The example has to do with a fact. If the sentence were changed slightly, choice (A) would be correct: "Er kennt mich." Now it has to do with knowing me and not simply with knowing my name. Other examples of the use of kennen:

Er kennt Berlin sehr gut.
He knows Berlin very well.
Kennst du den Roman von Hesse?
Are you acquianted with the novel by Hesse?

Choice (C) is the "du"-form of the verb "wissen." Choice (D) is the imperfect form of the verb "kennen."

33. (D)

"Jeder" has the same ending as the definite article. Since "Kind" is neuter and it is nominative in this sentence, the ending is -s (compare to the definite article: das). Choice (A) would be correct if the subject were masculine (compare to the definite article: der). Choice (B) is both of the wrong gender (masculine) and the wrong case (accusative). Choice (C) would be correct, if the subject were feminine (compare to the definite article: die).

34. (B)

"Sich lassen + Infinitive" means "to have_____ done". The sentence given here means "He is having his hair cut." Choice (A) is from the verb "sich verlassen". Used with the preposition "auf", it means "to depend upon". The non-reflexive form given in choice (C) means "to leave a place or person". Choice (D), from the verb "lassen", means "to allow."

Examples: Er verläßt sich auf mich. (He depends upon me.)
Er verläßt Berlin. (He is leaving Berlin.)

Er läßt die Kinder gehen. (He is letting the children go.)

35. (A)

The verb "gehören" takes a dative object. For this reason, choices (B), (C), and (D) are incorrect. They are all accusative forms.

36. (B)

The interrogative "welcher" has the same endings as the definite article. In order to arrive at the correct answer, you need to know that "Koffer" is masculine and that it is used here in the accusative case. Since the masculine accusative definite article is "den", the ending here is "-en". Choice (A) would be correct if it were the subject of the sentence. Choice (C) would be correct if "Koffer" were neuter. Choice (D) would be correct, if "Koffer" were feminine.

37. (D)

"Möchten" functions as a modal does. Therefore, there is no "zu" before the infinitive, as in choice (C). Choice (A) means "to lead" and doesn't fit logically. Choice (B) is a past participle and does not fit grammatically with the conjugated verb "möchte".

38. (C)

This is an unpreceded adjective. This means that no articles are before it. Unpreceded adjective endings follow the pattern of the definite article in all cases except the genitive masculine and neuter, which have the weak ending "-en". To arrive at the ending for unpreceded adjectives in all other cases, ask yourself what the definite article would be if you were to substitute it for the adjective. In this case, the definite article would be "die", since "sind" indicates that "Brötchen" is plural. Therefore, the ending is "-e". Answer (A) would be correct, if "Brötchen" were singular. Following the logic stated above, we could substitute the definite article "das" and arrive at the "-es" ending. Choice (B) seems logical, since all preceded plural adjective endings are "-en". However, this is not the case for unpreceded adjective endings. Again, they follow the pattern of the definite article. Choice (D) might sound best to a native speaker of English, because it has no ending. However, attributive adjectives in German always have endings.

39. (D)

The mother and daughter wanted to go shopping. Since the story states they were driving into the city, we can assume they did not live there, as stated in (A). It also states "wie sie es gewohnt waren" that they were accustomed to going shopping together. Therefore, answer (B) does not apply, since it states that they did this seldom. Since the mother was picking up the daughter, they did not live together in the city, as stated in (C).

40. (C)

The mother sometimes picked the daughter up. She was not picked up by the daughter, as stated in (A). She did pick her up, as stated in (B), but not because it was her habit. They took turns, and this time it was the mother's turn (Die Mutter war an der Reihe). Therefore, she did not always (immer) pick her up, as stated in (D).

41. (B)

On the way back, they saw a run-over dog in the street. They did not run over a dog in the street (A), nor did they run over a dead dog (C). They also did not see a run-over, but not yet dead, dog in the street (D).

42. (A)

The man placed the dog into the luggage compartment. He did not ask if it was their dog (B). He had not accidently run over the dog (C), nor did he want to bury it (D).

43. (B)

They became almost hysterical when they saw the dead dog. They did not cry for joy (B). They also did not believe "Waldi" was still at home (C), not did they want to leave the dog there (D).

44. (D)

Waldi was still sleeping in front of the house when the two women returned. It was not Waldi who needed to be buried, but the unknown dog (A). He was not buried by the man (B). Waldi was not happy when they arrived (C). He was still sleeping.

45. (A)

The American wanted to donate blood because she needed money. It is true that she was far away from her parents (B), but that is not the reason for her wish to donate blood. She did not want to donate blood because she was looking for a job (C), but because, as a foreigner, she was not allowed to work. She was not driven to sell her blood, because her friends did not WANT to help her (D). Perhaps they did want to, but were equally poor.

46. (C)

She could not look for a job, because foreigners are not allowed to work without permission, not because her parents were against it (A). It may be true that her friends did not work (B), but that does not explain why she could not. (D) states that she could borrow money from her friends. That is not the case.

47. (B)

The student only understood part of what the medic said, not everything, as stated in choice (A). (C) states that she understood nothing. Choice (D) states that she understood exactly (genau) what he said.

48. (B)

The medic did not pay attention to what she was doing, because he was busy. His lack of attention had nothing to do with her need of money (B). He did not neglect her because he was trying to control himself (C), or because he was laughing (D).

49. (C)

The student undressed, because she had misunderstood, not because the doctor told her to (A). It was also not because she did not want to hesitate (B). The doctor did say it slowly and clearly (D), but only after she had undressed.

50. (A)

The actors in the German Theater in Hamburg are looking for a run-away dog. They are not looking for a man, who is one of their main actors (B). They are also not looking for a sheep dog, who is playing the role of Aaron (C). Choice (D) states that they are looking for a dog, who COULD play a role in a play by Shakespeare. This is not true. They are looking for Aaron, who DOES play a role in a play by Shakespeare.

51. (B)

Aaron disappeared during a walk. He did not get lost driving to Bavaria (A). He did not get lost because he wanted to run through the woods alone (C). He was chasing a female dog. He also did not get lost, because he wanted to vacation in Bavaria (D).

52. (B)

He ran away, because he fell in love, not because he didn't want to work anymore (A), or because he wanted to disappear (C). It was also not because he wanted to go on (D).

53. (D)

Not only his owner, but also the actors are hoping he will return. Therefore (A) is incorrect. It states that only his owner is interested in whether or not he returns. Choice (B) states that only a spokesperson for the theater is hoping for his return. (C) says that only a shepherd is worried.

54. (D)

Aaron and Sissy are a strange pair, because they look different. It is not because Aaron is an actor (A), or because Sissy is not an actress (B).

It also has nothing to do with the fact that Aaron is too passionate (C).

55. (B)

"Wußte" is the imperfect form of the verb "wissen". Choice (A) does not exist. It is the present tense form with a past tense ending. Choice (C) is the subjunctive II form and does not fit the context of the sentence, since there is no contrary-to-fact condition expressed. Choice (D) is the past participle of the verb "wissen" and does not fit grammatically.

56. (A)

There are three ways to say "where" in German. "Woher" means literally "from where" and must be used when that is the sense of the message. "Wo" has nothing to do with motion and is used when simply talking about location. The verb "kommen" in this sentence makes clear that that is not the case here. Therefore, choice (B) is incorrect. "Wohin" literally means "where to" and must be used when the motion is away from the speaker. Therefore, choice (C) is incorrect. Choice (D) looks as if it had to do with "where", but it means "what for". Examples of the use of wo, wohin, and woher:

Wo bist du? Where are you?
Wohin gehst du? Where are you going?
Woher kommst du? Where are you from?

57. (A)

"Feststellen" is a verb that has a separable prefix. In a main clause, as here, the prefix (fest) goes to the end of the main clause. This explains why choice (B) is incorrect. Choice (C) is incorrect, because the "ge-" prefix of the past participle should be between the prefix and the rest of the verb: festgestellt. Choice (D) is incorrect, because it does not fit into the context of the sentence. It is a passive form and the meaning of the verb "feststellen", "to establish, to find out", makes it impossible to have a person as its subject in the passive.

58. (A)

Because of the preposition "aus", "dem gleichen Stadtteil" is in the dative case. The dative ending of all adjectives that are preceded by other adjectives ("gleichen" is preceded by "dem" in this case), whether preceded by the definite or indefinite and regardless of gender, is "-en". For this reason, choices (B), (C), and (D) are incorrect.

59. (B)

A basic rule of German word order is that the verb occupies the second position in a sentence. This rule applies here. The adverb "gestern' is considered the first element in the sentence, and the verb must follow. For this reason, all of the other choices are incorrect.

60. (A)

"In" is a preposition which can have a dative object, if there is no motion toward a goal, as is the case here, or an accusative object, if there is motion toward a goal. One must also know that "Bibliothek" is feminine in order to answer the question correctly. The feminine dative definite article is "der". Choice (B) is in the wrong case (accusative). Choice (C) is of the wrong gender (masculine or neuter), and choice (D) is the wrong case (accusative) and gender (masculine).

61. (D)

In an indirect question, "if" is expressed by "ob". Choice (A) is incorrect, because this in an indirect question and if the speaker is trying to ask "when" I have read something by Hesse, he would have to use "wann", and not "wenn". Choice (B) means "although" and does not make sense in this context. The same can be said for choice (C), which means "whom".

62. (D)

Normally the conjugated verb goes to the end of a subordinate clause. However, when there is a double infinitive in the present of past perfect tense, the conjugated verb is located immediately before the double infinitive. This explains why choice (A) is incorrect. Choice (B) is incorrect for the same reason, but it also has the incorrect form of "haben" to agree with the subject "ich". The latter is also true of choice (C), which does have the correct word order.

63. (C)

A contrary-to-fact subjunctive II form is used here, since I did NOT tell him to come again tomorrow. Since "sagen" forms its perfect tenses with "haben", we need the subjunctive II form of "haben". The proper subjunctive II form of a verb is arrived at in two ways. If a verb is a "weak" verb, that is, if one has to, when forming the imperfect form of the verb, add "t" to the verb stem and then add person inflections (e.g.: "ich kaufe" is "ich kaufte" in the imperfect), then the subjunctive II form of the verb is merely the same as the imperfective form (e.g.: "ich kaufe" is "ich kaufte" in the subjunctive II). However, if a verb is a "strong" verb, that is, if it has an irregular imperfective form, then the subjunctive II form of the verb is formed by taking the stem of the imperfective first person plural form, adding an umlaut to the stem (if possible), and then adding the endings -e, -est, -e, -en, -et, and -en (whichever is appropriate) to the modified stem. Thus, "ich komme" is "ich käme" (kam-käm-käme) in subjunctive II, and "ich habe" is "ich hätte" (hatte-hätte) in subjunctive II (haben is a rather irregular example of the formation of subjunctive).

Choice (C) is subjunctive II, but it is from "sein". Choice (B) is not a subjunctive II form. Choice (D) is also not a subjunctive form.

64. (C)

The person to whom one says something in German is in the dative case. It corresponds to English "to me, you, him" etc. Choice (A) is in the nominative and is incorrect. Choice (B) is accusative. Choice (D) can either be nominative or accusative.

65. (A)

This is an example of the subjunctive I. It is used in indirect discourse. That is the case here. The speaker is relating what he would have said. The subjunctive I is based on the present tense of the "wir" form. The endings are the same as the subjunctive II endings and are best remembered by learning the endings of the imperfective form of "arbeiten" after the -t: ich arbeitetE, du arbeitetEST, er arbeitetE, wir arbeitetEN, ihr arbeitetET, sie arbeitetEN.

Wir müssen (present) → er arbeitetE → er müsse.

Choice (B) is the "ihr" present tense form of müssen. Choice (C) is either the infinitive or the "wir"-, "sie"-, or "sie"-form. Choice (D) is the "du"-form in the present tense.

66. (D)

Since the conjugated verb is a modal (müsse), the verb at the end is an infinitive. There is no "zu" before the infinitive when the conjugated verb is a modal. For this reason, choices (B) and (C) are wrong. Choice (A) would occur in a main clause with a plural subject, such as: Sie kommen wieder.

67. (D)

"Nachdem" is a subordinating conjunction, and therefore it causes the conjugated verb to go to the end of the phrase. For this reason, choice (C) is incorrect. It is immediately followed by the subject. Therefore, choices (A) and (B) are wrong. So, the word order in a "nachdem" clause is:

Nachdem	subject	conjugated verb.
1	2	end

68. (B)

Since "nachdem" means "after", the following clause cannot be in the present tense. Therefore, choice (A) is wrong. Choice (C) is present subjunctive II and does not fit grammatically or logically. Choice (D) does not exist.

69. (A)

With only a few exceptions, the preposition "to", before the name of a place, is "nach" in German. The exceptions have to do with countries having the definite article, such as "die Schweiz" (Switzerland), "die Soviet Union," "die Turkei". For example:

Er fährt in die Schweiz.
He is going to Switzerland.

Since Köln has no article, choice (B) is wrong. Choices (C) and (D) would not be possible in this context. Choice (C) does mean "to" and is used before personal pronouns: Er kommt zu mir. (He is coming to [see] me. Choice (D) often means "at the home of" or "at ____ house." For example: Er wohnt bei mir. (He lives at my house/with me.)

70. (A)

"Wird zugemacht" is the present passive. It means "is closed". There is always a form of the verb "werden" in the passive:

Das Fenster wird zugemacht.
(The window is [being] closed.)
Das Fenster wurde zugemacht.
(The window was [being] closed.)
Das Fenster ist zugemacht worden.
(The window was [being] closed.)
Das Fenster war zugemacht worden.
(The window had been closed.)
Das Fenster wird zugemacht werden.
(The window will be closed.)

"Worden" exists only to form the perfect tenses of the passive. Choice (B) is called a "false" passive. It appears to be the passive, but it isn't, since it doesn't describe an action, but a state: The window is [in the state of being] closed. "Zugemacht" in choice (B) is an adjective, not a past participle. The passive always describes an action. Choice (C) does not exist. The subjunctive form "wurde" is followed by an infinitive, not a past participle.

71. (D)

This is an example of the subjunctive "würde" + infinitive construction. It means "would . . .break/be destroyed". Choice (A) is the past perfect and means "had broken". It does not fit the context of the sentence. Choice (B) would be possible if the "ware" had an umlaut. In that case, the sentence would mean: The window is closed everyday, otherwise everything would be broken. Choice (C) is the present perfect tense. It means "was . . . broken" and does not fit.

72. (A)

The young couple went through an attic window without difficulty. They did not go through the royal kitchen (B). They did climb up construction scaffolding (Baugerüst), but did not find a door (C). They did not look through an attic window until no one was in the kitchen (D).

73. (C)

From all evidence, they felt very much at home in the palace. They were not afraid (A). They did dare to help themselves to exotic Chinese delicacies in the kitchen (B). They did not want to leave right away (D), but spent the night.

74. (D)

The former art students were caught, because they decided to take along some paintings as souvenirs, not because they wanted to take a bath (A), or eat (B), or sleep (C).

75. (A)

The night was expensive, because they had to pay a fine (eine Strafe bezahlen). It was almost twice as expensive as a night in the most expensive hotel in Amsterdam, not ALMOST as expensive as a hotel (B) or cheaper than in an expensive hotel (C), or as expensive as a hotel (D).

76. (A)

The sponsors (Veranstalter) of "Butter-und Kaffee-" trips want to sell products. They are not interested in offering excursions at low prices (A), nor do they wish to give pleasure (ein Vergnügen bereiten) to the participants (C). Even the sponsors of "Butter" trips are not chiefly interested in selling butter. being able to buy butter at duty-free prices is a side attraction. "Kaffee" trips have nothing to do with buying coffee. Stopping at a cafe is usually one of the attractions, but the main purpose is to demonstrate products for sale at higher prices than those in stores (D).

77. (B)

The difference between "Kaffee" and "Butter" trips is that a "Butter" trip always includes an ocean excursion. That explains the duty-free butter prices. A "Butter" trip is not necessarily cheaper than a "Kaffee" trip (D). Answers (A) and (C) are explained in the solution to problem 76.

78. (B)

The advantage of such excursions is that one can have a nice trip at a low price -- if one does not fall into the trap of spending a lot of money on overpriced products. One could conceivably indeed buy lots of Butter and Kaffee (A), but that isn't the real advantage of such trips. It is not the case that one can always buy products at favorable prices (C). Only the duty-free products are inexpensive and they are only available on a "Butter" excursion. One cannot travel for nothing (umsonst) (D). There is a fee for both "Kaffee" and "Butter" trips, but these fees are very low.

79. (D)

The disadvantage of "Kaffee" and "Butter" excursions is that the products shown and demonstrated are expensive. It might also be true that the trips are long and tiring (A), but that isn't discussed in this reading. It might also be true that the coffee isn't good (B), but we aren't told that here. It probably isn't true that the butter is expensive (C), since it is duty-free.

80. (C)

Those who can profit most from these trips are the ones who can resist the temptation (der Versuchung widerstehen) to purchase the expensive products. Those who have a lot of money (B) will not profit. They might unnecessarily spend their money on products they could get more inexpensively elsewhere. Those who have little money and still buy the expensive products (A) will profit least of all. The same can be said for those who buy everything offered, whether of good value (preiswert) or not (D).

GERMAN TEST V

PART A

Time: 1 Hour
80 Questions

DIRECTIONS: Each of the sentences in this part has a blank space indicating that a word or phrase has been omitted. From the four choices select the ONE that when inserted in the sentence fits grammatically and logically with the sentence as a whole. Then blacken the corresponding space on the answer sheet.

1. Peter spricht mit der Frau, ... er gestern getroffen hat.

(A) wem
(B) die
(C) was
(D) der

2. Das ist die ... Kirche, die ich je gesehen habe.

(A) schönsten
(B) schönster
(C) schönste
(D) schönstes

3. Meine Schwester hat den Film nicht sehen ... .

(A) können
(B) gekonnt
(C) haben
(D) worden

4. Im dritten Geschäft haben wir endlich ... Erdbeeren gefunden.

(A) frischen
(B) frischer
(C) frischen
(D) frische

5. Von diesem Schauspieler habe ich noch nie ... .

(A) hören
(B) gehören
(C) hörte
(D) gehört

6. Alle meine Freunde gehen nachmittags in ... Garten.

(A) das
(B) dem
(C) der
(D) den

7. Obwohl es gefährlich war, sprang Jürgen auf den ... Zug.

(A) fahrend
(B) gefahren
(C) fahrenden
(D) fahren

8. Inge sagte, sie ... ihre Hausaufgaben nicht gemacht.

(A) habe
(B) würde
(C) sei
(D) hätte

9. Warum trägst du immer die Kleider … Schwester?

(A) deines
(B) deinem
(C) deinen
(D) deiner

10. … wurde nichts von dem Unfall gesagt.

(A) er
(B) ihm
(C) ihn
(D) sie

11. Ich fahre lieber mit meinem eigenen Auto. Du fährst immer so … .

(A) schnellsten
(B) schnell
(C) schnelleres
(D) schnellem

12. Im Krankenhaus habe ich viele Leute mit … Armen gesehen.

(A) brechender
(B) brechen
(C) gebrochenen
(D) bricht

13. Vielleicht kann er es morgen noch einmal … .

(A) versuchen
(B) versucht
(C) versuchte
(D) zu versuchen

14. Das Glas, aus ... ich getrunken habe, war nicht sauber.

(A) das
(B) wem
(C) der
(D) dem

15. Morgen ... Dieter noch einmal kommen.

(A) werden
(B) wird
(C) wurde
(D) geworden

16. Der Ober ... Schnitzel mit Kartoffelsalat.

(A) empfehlt
(B) empfehlte
(D) empfiehlt
(D) empfehlen

17. In der Loge klatschte ... begeistert.

(A) jemand
(B) jemandem
(C) jemanden
(D) jemandes

18. Das Geld ... von den Einbrechern gestohlen worden.

(A) ist
(B) wird
(C) sind
(D) hat

19. Wegen ... Regens hat die Fahrt länger gedauert.

(A) dem
(B) der
(C) die
(D) des

20. Die Zugspitze ist der ... Berg Deutschlands.

(A) höhere
(B) hohe
(C) am höchsten
(D) höchste

PART B

DIRECTIONS: The sentences below contain blank spaces indicating omissions in the text. Below each blank are four choices. Select the choice that is grammatically correct in the context and blacken the corresponding space on the answer sheet. Be sure to read the sentences first.

21. Mein Freund wohnt ... 20 Jahren im gleichen Haus.

(A) vor
(B) nach
(C) seit
(D) für

22. Das Theaterstück von Brecht hat ... sehr gut gefallen.

(A) unser
(B) mir
(C) mich
(D) ihre

23. Der Lehrer wartete schon lange … .

(A) darauf
(B) auf es
(C) dagegen
(D) womit

24. … Goethe 1794 nach Italien reiste, besuchte er auch Rom.

(A) wenn
(B) als
(C) wann
(D) ob

25. Im November werden die Nächte immer … .

(A) am längsten
(B) lang
(C) länger
(D) mehr lang

26. Das darf … nicht wahr sein!

(A) denn
(B) schon
(C) doch
(D) mal

27. Wir fahren heute nicht nach München, … nach Salzburg.

(A) sondern
(B) weil
(C) aber
(D) denn

28. Seit meinem letzten Besuch ... ich Deutschland sehr gut.

(A) weiss
(B) verstehe
(D) kenne
(D) mag

29. Nach langem Nachdenken hat er endlich eine ... getroffen.

(A) Meinung
(B) Frage
(C) Entscheidung
(D) Antwort

30. Bei diesem kalten Wetter kann man ... leicht erkälten.

(A) sich
(B) mich
(C) mir
(D) uns

31. Ich spiele manchmal Fussball, aber ... Basketball interessiere ich mich überhaupt nicht.

(A) für
(B) über
(C) in
(D) mit

32. Vor ... Dingen braucht meine Schwester immer Geld.

(A) jeden
(B) ersten
(C) keinen
(D) allen

33. Das Schillerdenkmal wurde vor 200 Jahren ... .

(A) errichtet
(B) gelesen
(C) gekauft
(D) gefunden

34. Meine Eltern hätten gerne ein neues Haus, aber sie können es ... .

(A) nicht verkaufen
(B) sich nicht leisten
(C) erst nächste Woche sehen
(D) von der Bank bekommen

35. Weil Jürgen noch ein kleines Kind ist, soll er immer den Mund ... .

(A) aufmachen
(B) öffnen
(C) halten
(D) zeigen

36. Ich gehe ins Kino. Du kannst das Auto waschen ... .

(A) dürfen
(B) lassen
(C) mögen
(D) müssen

37. Je früher wir aufstehen, ... früher kommen wir an.

(A) trotz
(B) um zu
(C) aber
(D) desto

38. Meine Frau kommt immer zu spät, da ihre Uhr … .

(A) vorrennt
(B) vorläuft
(C) vorgeht
(D) vorkommt

39. Wenn du mir nicht geholfen hättest, … hätte ich es nie geschafft.

(A) dann
(B) wann
(C) denn
(D) danach

40. Eltern lieben ihre Kinder, obwohl sie … .

(A) gute Noten in der Schule haben
(B) gerne mit ihnen spielen
(C) ihnen oft Sorgen machen
(D) immer auf ihre Eltern hören

PART C

DIRECTIONS: The sentences below contain blank spaces indicating omissions in the text. Below each blank are four choices. Select the choice that is grammatically correct in the context and blacken the corresponding space on the answer sheet. Be sure to read the sentences first.

You have to connect **Questions 41** and **42.**

41. Er ist nicht … ,

(A) laufen
(B) geantwortet
(C) geblieben
(D) fuhr

42. weil er keine ... mehr hatte.

(A) Zeit
(B) Hunger
(C) Bier
(D) Uhr

Questions 43–45 are connected with each other. The indefinite pronoun at the beginning of **Question 44** refers to **Question 43.**

43. ... Sommer fahren wir immer ans Meer.

(A) Zum
(B) Im
(C) Während
(D) Auf

44. Das ist ... für die Kinder schön,

(A) denn
(B) nie
(C) kaum
(D) besonders

45. denn sie ... dann immer am Strand spielen.

(A) müssen
(B) können
(C) sollen
(D) werden

Questions 46–48 are connected. They all make statements about the German soccer-player Franz Beckenbauer.

46. Franz Beckenbauer war ein ... Fussballspieler.

(A) schöne
(B) bekanntes
(C) berühmter
(D) alten

47. Viele Leute sprechen noch heute über ... .

(A) ihn
(B) sie
(C) es
(D) uns

48. Sie können ihn einfach nicht ... .

(A) überreden
(B) versuchen
(C) vergessen
(D) unternehmen

Questions 49–51 are one sentence.

49. Ich habe den Entschluss ... ,

(A) gefasst
(B) gemacht
(C) gehört
(D) geschrieben

50. mit dem Rauchen ... ,

(A) aufhören
(B) aufgehört
(C) aufzuhören
(D) zu aufhören

51. aber ich weiss, es wird ... nicht leichtfallen.

(A) mich
(B) mir
(C) ich
(D) mein

Questions 52–54 form a single sentence. You have to understand the meaning of the whole sentence in order to answer correctly.

52. Das Buch, das ich gestern gelesen ... ,

(A) bin
(B) haben
(C) werde
(D) habe

53. war sehr ... ,

(A) romantisches
(B) romantische
(C) romantisch
(D) romantischer

54. ... nicht besonders spannend.

(A) denn
(B) sondern
(C) jedoch
(D) jedenfalls

Questions 55–57 are connected.

55. Ich freue mich immer besonders ... Weihnachten,

(A) zu
(B) nach
(C) auf
(D) in

56. weil ... dann die ganze Familie versammelt,

(A) uns
(B) sich
(C) euch
(D) mich

57. und wir uns so wenigstens einmal im Jahr unterhalten ... .

(A) konnten
(B) könnten
(C) gekonnt
(D) können

58. Im letzten Monat hat mein Mann ... verdient als sonst,

(A) am meisten
(B) viel
(C) mehr
(D) meistens

59. weil er ... Überstunden gamacht hat,

(A) viel
(B) viele
(C) vielen
(D) vieles

60. ... er sonst nie tut.

(A) das
(B) wie
(C) die
(D) was

PART D

DIRECTIONS: Read the following passages carefully for comprehension. Each passage is followed by a number of incomplete statements or questions. Select the completion or answer that is best according to the passage and blacken the corresponding space on the answer sheet.

Das Deutsche Reich von 1871 war Bismarcks Reich. Bismarck ist oft als einer der wichtigsten Persönlichkeiten der deutschen Geschichte bezeichnet worden. Sein Hauptinteresse galt der Aussenpolitik, während die Innenpolitik mehr von den Parlamenten bestimmt wurde. Zeit seines Lebens blieb Bismarck ein Monarchist, der die Parlamente nur als notwendiges Übel ansah, und der versuchte, sie für seine Zwecke zu benutzen.

Bismarcks grösste innenpolitische Erfolge waren die Gründung des deutschen Reiches, die Vermeidung der Revolution, sowie die Einführung der Sozialversicherung für Arbeiter. Seine grössten innenpolitischen Probleme bestanden im sogenannten Kulturkampf zwischen Katholiken und Protestanten und dem Aufkommen der Sozialisten, die Bismarck als gefährlich für den Staat betrachtete.

Aussenpolitisch muss Bismarcks Hauptleistung wohl darin gesehen werden, zuerst Preussen und dann das Deutsche Reich neben Frankreich, England und Russland zu einer Grossmacht in Europa gemacht zu haben. Allerdings wird von vielen Historikern behauptet, dass Bismarcks Aussenpolitik den Grundstein für den 1. Weltkrieg gelegt hat.

61. Die Absicht des Autors ist

(A) zu zeigen, dass Aussen- und Innenpolitik für Bismarck gleich wichtig waren

(B) die politischen Leistungen Bismarcks kurz darzustellen
(C) Bismarck als Monarchisten zu diffamieren
(D) die Behauptung aufzustellen, dass Bismarck eine der grössten Gestalten der deutschen Geschichte war

62. Aus dem Text kann man schliessen, dass Bismarck

(A) Sozialist war
(B) den Kulturkampf entschieden hat
(C) eine Revolution wollte
(D) Parlamente nicht mochte

63. Bismarcks Aussenpolitik hatte zum Ziel,

(A) Frankreich, England und Russland zu besiegen
(B) Deutschland mit Frankreich, England und Russland gleichzustellen
(C) den Kulturkampf in Frankreich, England und Russland zu beenden
(D) die Monarchie in Frankreich, England und Russland zu erhalten

Die Brüder Thomas und Heinrich Mann gehören beide zu den bekanntesten deutschen Dichtern des 20. Jahrhunderts. Von Thomas kennt man besonders die Romane "Buddenbrooks," "Der Zauberberg" und "Doktor Faustus," von Heinrich die Romane "Der Untertan" und "Professor Unrat."

Das Verhältnis der Brüder zueinander war nicht immer einfach und oft von Missverständnissen und Eifersucht geprägt. Die gegenseitige Entfremdung hatte begonnen, als Thomas seinen Bruder in einem Aufsatz einen "Zivilisationsliteraten" nannte. Der Begriff war eine Anspielung auf Heinrichs Hochachtung vor der französischen Kultur und Literatur, die Thomas geringschätzte.

Während Heinrich Zeit seines Lebens ein begeisterter Demokrat war, hatte Thomas Schwierigkeiten, nach dem Zusammenbruch des Kaiserreiches 1918 die sogenannte "Weimarer Republik" zu unterstützen. Erst langsam kämpfte er sich in den zwanziger Jahren zu einer vorsichtigen Befürwortung der Demokratie durch. Heinrich hingegen liebte die Republik und wurde sogar als Präsidentschaftskandidat der Sozialdemokraten vorgeschlagen.

Nach der Machtergreifung Hitlers im Jahre 1933 mussten sowohl Thomas als auch Heinrich Mann in die USA auswandern. In der Emigration verschlechterte sich ihr Verhältnis noch mehr, weil Thomas inzwischen berühmter als Heinrich war, und Thomas deshalb in finanzieller Unabhängigkeit leben konnte, während Heinrich arm und zeitweilig auf Hilfe vom Bruder angewiesen war.

Nach 1945 kehrten die Bruder Mann nach Europa zurück. Thomas liess sich zunächst in der Schweiz nieder, und Heinrich ging in die DDR, wo man ihn als Nationaldichter feierte. Im Alter verstanden sich die Brüder etwas besser, zu einer vollständigen Versöhnung kam es jedoch nie.

64. Die Brüder Thomas und Heinrich Mann

(A) haben sich immer gestritten
(B) haben sich sehr geliebt
(C) hatten ein schwieriges Verhältnis zueinander
(D) haben einige Romane zusammen geschrieben

65. Die Jahre zwischen 1933 und 1945 verbrachten Thomas und Heinrich in

(A) der Schweiz
(B) der DDR
(C) Amerika
(D) Frankreich

66. Das Leben Heinrich Manns war

(A) typisch für einen Zivilisationsliteraten
(B) wie das vieler Präsidentschaftskandidaten
(C) eng mit dem seines Bruders verbunden
(D) durch den Zusammenbruch des Kaiserreiches im Jahre 1918 gekennzeichnet

67. Die politischen Überzeugungen der Brüder Mann waren

(A) einander ähnlich
(B) unterschiedlich
(C) völlig dieselben
(D) reaktionär

Der deutsche Mieterbund hat in seiner Zeitschrift darauf hingewiesen, dass ein Mieter nicht haftbar gemacht werden kann, wenn er vor seinem Fernseher einschläft und daraus ein Schaden entsteht.

Die Mieter-Zeitung berichtete von einem Fall, bei dem ein Fernsehgerät in Brand geriet, nachdem sein Besitzer eingenickt war. Der Vermieter der Wohnung verlangte Schadenersatz in Höhe von 61.000 Mark, da er sich nicht hoch genug versichert hatte und in seinem Haus ein hoher Schaden durch den Brand verursacht worden war. Er behauptete, dass der Besitzer des Fernsehers für sein Gerät verantwortlich sei und keinesfalls vor ihm einschlafen dürfe.

Ein Gericht in Köln stimmte dem Argument des Vermieters jedoch nicht zu, und es vertrat die Auffassung, dass ein Fernseher beim heutigen Stand der Technik nicht besonders bewacht werden müsse. Ausserdem sei es bei der Qualität vieler Fernsehsendungen kein Wunder, dass mehr und mehr Zuschauer Schwierigkeiten hätten, wach zu bleiben, fügte der Richter in seinem Urteilsspruch hinzu.

68. In Deutschland werden offenbar

(A) einige Brände durch Fernseher verursacht
(B) Häuser oft in Brand gesteckt
(C) alle Fernseher automatisch ausgeschaltet, wenn sein Besitzer einschläft
(D) wie durch ein Wunder die Fernsehprogramme immer schlechter

69. Fernseher haben heute einen so hohen technischen Stand, dass

(A) man nicht auf sie aufpassen muss
(B) sie keinesfalls Brände verursachen können
(C) sie manchmal bis zu 61.000 Mark kosten
(D) die Zuschauer oft nicht einschlafen können

70. Der Richter meint, dass manche Fernsehsendungen

(A) ausgezeichnet sind
(B) langweilig sind
(C) spannend sind
(D) qualitativ sind

71. Der deutsche Mieterbund

(A) vertritt die Ansicht, dass der Besitzer des Fernsehers für den Brand verantwortlich ist
(B) berichtet über einen interessanten Gerichtsfall
(C) findet, dass niemand vor seinem Fernseher einschlafen sollte
(D) kritisiert das Urteil des Gerichtes in Köln

72. Der Vermieter will

(A) eine neue Versicherung
(B) seine Verluste erstattet bekommen
(C) einen neuen Fernseher
(D) Schadenersatz von der Mieter-Zeitung

Ärzte der chirurgischen Universitätsklinik Münster haben in einer Untersuchung herausgefunden, dass vielleicht noch vor dem Jahr 2000 mehr Frauen an Herzinfarkten, Lungenkrebs und anderen "Männerkrankheiten" sterben werden als Männer. Diese erstaunliche Entwicklung würde dann dazu führen, dass die Lebenserwartung der Frauen unter die der Männer sinken würde.

Dr. Dittrich, der Direktor der Klinik, sagte in einem Interview: "Die Frau holt in jeder Beziehung auf. Immer mehr junge Frauen kommen mit Herzinfarkten, Bronchialkarzinomen und sogar Raucherbeinen ins Krankenhaus."

Was sind die Gründe für diesen Trend? Dr. Dittrich erläuterte, dass man fast weltweit beobachten könne, wie Frauen versuchen würden, den männlichen Lebensstil zu übrernehmen. Wie dieses "verrückte" Verhalten der Frauen zu erklären sei, wisse man noch nicht genau. Einige Psychologen meinen, dass viele Frauen offenbar als Folge der Emanzipation ein so starkes seelisches Nachholbedürfnis hätten, so leben zu wollen wie Männer, dass sie ihre Gesundheit rücksichtslos gefährdeten.

73. Ärzte der Universitätsklinik Münster haben herausgefunden, dass

(A) Männerkrankheiten eigentlich Frauenkrankheiten sind
(B) heute mehr Frauen an Herzinfarkten sterben als Männer
(C) bis zum Jahr 2000 Frauen kaum an Herzinfarkten sterben werden
(D) die Zahl der Frauen, die an Herzinfarkten sterben, zunimmt

74. Dr. Dittrich stellte fest, dass

(A) mehr junge als alte Frauen mit Herzinfarkten ins Krankenhaus kommen
(B) mehr junge Frauen als früher Herzinfarkte bekommen
(C) Frauen heute mehr Beziehungen als früher haben und deshalb mehr Herzinfarkte erleiden
(D) mehr Frauen mit Raucherbeinen als mit Bronchialkarzinomen ins Krankenhaus kommen

75. Ein Grund für die in dem Artikel beschriebene Entwicklung ist möglicherweise

(A) eine Senkung der Lebenserwartung der Frauen
(B) die Übernahme des männlichen Lebensstiles durch Frauen
(C) ein Anstieg der Zahl der Frauen
(D) die immer noch nicht vollständig vollzogene Emanzipation der Frau

76. Die Wissenschaftler halten diese Entwicklung für

(A) bemerkenswert
(B) gut
(C) unwichtig
(D) beispielhaft

In Hessen hat die Polizei Falschgeld sichergestellt, das mit Hilfe eines Farbkopierers hergestellt wurde. Es ist das erste Mal, dass es der Polizei gelungen ist, nachzuweisen, dass ein solch neuartiges Gerät zum Vervielfältigen der "Blüten," wie man Falschgeld auch oft nennt, benutzt wurde.

Das Kriminalamt in Wiesbaden war auf die Spur einer 34-jährigen Frau gekommen, als sie versuchte, mit einer zunächst täuschend echt wirkenden 500-Mark-Note ein Paar Damenstrümpfe zu kaufen. Die Kassiererin nahm den Schein zunächst an, wurde aber später unsicher und notierte sich die Autonummer der Kundin. Das Kennzeichen führte die Polizei schliesslich zu der Wohnung des 38-jährigen Freundes der Frau. Dort wurde der Farbkopierer, der zur Vervielfältigung des Falschgeldes benutzt worden war, sichergestellt.

Ob das Paar die Idee, "Blüten" mit Hilfe eines Farbkopierers in Umlauf zu bringen, alleine hatte, oder ob noch andere Täter die gleiche Methode gebrauchen, konnte von der Polizei zur Zeit noch nicht festgestellt werden.

77. Die Herstellung von Falschgeld mit einem Farbkopierer ist

(A) schon seit längerer Zeit üblich
(B) unmöglich
(C) die neueste Methode, Falschgeld herzustellen
(D) in Hessen legalisiert worden

78. Das Autokennzeichen der Frau war

(A) eine Spur, die der Polizei half
(B) gefälscht
(C) eine "Blüte"
(D) von der Kassiererin nicht angenommen worden

79. Die Kassiererin

(A) hatte die 500-Mark-Note mit einem Farbkopierer hergestellt
(B) geistesgegenwärtig das Richtige getan
(C) die 500-Mark-Note sofort als "Blüte" erkannt
(D) die Polizei zur Wohnung des Freundes der Frau geführt

80. Die Polizei untersucht noch,

(A) wer die Kundin war
(B) wie das Falschgeld hergestellt wurde
(C) ob der 500-Mark-Schein echt war
(D) ob noch andere Personen Farbkopierer für Fälschungen benutzen

THE COLLEGE BOARD ACHIEVEMENT TEST IN GERMAN

TEST V

ANSWER KEY

1.	B	21.	D	41.	C	61.	B
2.	C	22.	B	42.	A	62.	D
3.	A	23.	A	43.	C	63.	B
4.	D	24.	A	44.	D	64.	C
5.	D	25.	C	45.	B	65.	C
6.	B	26.	C	46.	C	66.	C
7.	C	27.	A	47.	A	67.	B
8.	A	28.	C	48.	C	68.	A
9.	D	29.	C	49.	A	69.	A
10.	B	30.	A	50.	C	70.	B
11.	B	31.	A	51.	B	71.	B
12.	C	32.	D	52.	D	72.	B
13.	A	33.	A	53.	C	73.	D
14.	D	34.	B	54.	C	74.	B
15.	B	35.	B	55.	D	75.	B
16.	C	36.	B	56.	B	76.	A
17.	A	37.	D	57.	D	77.	C
18.	A	38.	C	58.	C	78.	A
19.	D	39.	A	59.	B	79.	B
20.	D	40.	C	60.	D	80.	D

GERMAN TEST V DETAILED EXPLANATIONS OF ANSWERS

1. (B)

This question examines your mastery of the relative pronouns. In German, the number and the gender of a relative pronoun are determined by the word the relative pronoun refers back to (here: "die Frau"), and its case is determined by the function (i.e. Subject, Accusative, or Dative Object) the relative pronoun has in the relative clause. "Die Frau" is Neuter and Singular, and the relative pronoun is the Accusative object of the relative clause. Therefore, you must choose the Neuter, Singular, Accusative relative pronoun, which is "die" (Choice (B)). Choice (A) is wrong, since German uses definite articles (i.e. "der," "die," "das") as relative pronouns, and not, like English, interrogative pronouns (i.e. "who," "whom"). The relative pronoun "was" (choice (C)) is only used when the whole main clause is referred back to. Choice (D) is incorrect, because "der" is the pronoun which had to be used if the relative pronoun were the Dative object of the relative clause.

2. (C)

In this question you are asked to find the proper adjective ending. First you have to determine whether an adjective is preceded by a "der-word" or an "ein-word," or whether it is unpreceded. Here it is preceded by "die," which is a "der-word." If an adjective is preceded by a "der-word," it always takes a weak ending. There are only two weak adjective-endings: -e and -en (Choices (A) and (C)). Choices (B) and (D), -er and -es, both represent strong endings and, therefore, are incorrect. In order to choose between the two possible endings, you have to recognize the gender, number, and the case of the noun, which is modified by the adjective (here: "Kirche"). "Kirche" is Singular and Feminine, and its case is Nominative, since the verb "ist" combines a subject with a predicate noun ("die Kirche"), which is also Nominative. The proper weak ending for a Feminine, Singular, Nominative adjective is -e (Choice (C)).

3. (A)

You are asked to determine the proper completion for a sentence that contains "hat" as its auxiliary verb and an infinitive ("sehen"). The only possible construction in which this could be the case is the Present Perfect of a Modal Auxiliary verb. Neither "haben" (Choice (C)) nor "worden" (Choice (D)) are Modals, which means that neither one is the correct answer. You have to know that German uses a double Infinitive in the Present Perfect for Modals and not, as with all other verbs, a Past Participle. Therefore, the Past Participle of the Modal "können" ("gekonnt") is wrong, and the correct answer is Choice (A).

4. (D)

You have to find the proper ending for an adjective that modifies the noun "Erdbeeren." You have to decide whether the noun is preceded by an "ein-word," a "der-word," or whether it is unpreceded. Here it is unpreceded, which means that it has to take a strong ending. The next step is to determine the case, the gender, and the number of the noun "Erdbeeren." It is Plural and Accusative. The Accusative Plural strong adjective ending is -e, and the correct Choice is (D).

5. (D)

You are requested to find the proper form of the verb "hören" to complete the sentence. The auxiliary verb "habe" indicates that the tense of the verb is the Present Perfect. The correct verb compliment for the Present Perfect is a Past Participle. Choice (A) offers the Infinitive and Choice (C) the Simple Past, which makes them both incorrect. In order to decide between Choices (B) and (D) you have to know that "hören" is a regular weak verb. These verbs form their Past Participle by adding a ge- prefix and -t to their stem. Therefore, Choice (D) is the correct answer.

6. (B)

The task is to find the correct definite article which is required by the preposition "in." "In" is a two-way preposition, which means it can either take the Accusative or the Dative. The verb determines which case a two-way preposition takes. If the verb indicates that the activity expressed takes place within a place, the preposition takes the Dative; if it indicates a change of place, it takes the Accusative. The verb "gehen" expresses a change of location, and the Accusative is required. Choices (B) and (C) both are Dative, and therefore incorrect. To determine the gender and the number of the article, you have to look at the gender and the number of the modified noun ("Garten"), which is Masculine Singular. The Masculine, Singular, Accusative definite article is "den" (Choice (B)).

7. (C)

This question requires you to determine that a Present Participle is needed to complete this sentence. A Present Participle is a verb used as an adjective and it expresses an activity that is presently performed by the noun it modifies (i.e. "the burning house"). German forms the Present Participle by adding -d to the Infinitive. Choice (B) gives the Past Participle of "fahren" and (D) the Infinitive.

Only Choices (A) and (C) are forms of the Present Participles. Since it is used here as a modifying adjective, it must take an ending in addition to the -d. Consequently, Choice (C) is the correct answer.

8. (A)

This sentence is an example of the usage of Indirect Speech. German uses a special Subjunctive for Indirect Speech, for which English no longer has an equivalent. Its forms are derived from the Present Tense stem of a verb. Furthermore, this sentence is in the Present Perfect, which requires the Past Tense Special Subjunctive. "Machen" takes "haben" as its auxiliary verb in the Present Perfect, therefore you have to choose the proper Special Subjunctive form of "haben." Choice (B) is the General Subjunctive of "werden," and Choice (C) the Special Subjunctive of "sein." Choice (D) offers the General Subjunctive of "haben." The right answer is Choice (A).

9. (D)

You are asked to find the correct possessive adjective which corresponds with the noun "Schwester." The phrase indicates a possession of the phrase "die Kleider." Therefore, its case is Genitive. "Schwester" is Singular and Feminine. Possessive adjectives are "ein-words," and the proper adjective-ending for a Genitive, Singular, Feminine "ein-word" is -er. The correct answer is Choice (D).

10. (B)

The verb form "wurde gesagt" indicates that the sentence is in the Passsive Voice. Translated into English, the sentence means "He was told nothing about the accident." It appears that literally translated into German, Choice (A) "er" would be the correct answer. However, you have to recognize that the Subject is based on the Dative Object of the Active Voice equivalent of this sentence ("Nothing was told to him about the accident"). Contrary to English, in German such a sentence retains the Dative object in the Dative when transferred into the Passive Voice. The only personal pronoun offered in the Dative is Choice (B), the correct answer.

11. (B)

You have to identify that the completion of this sentence must be an adverb. In German, only adjectives, which modify nouns, take endings. Choice (A) offers a Superlative ("the fastest") with a weak ending of the adjective "schnell;" Choice (C) the Comparative, which is inappropriate in connection with "immer so;" and Choice (D) a strong ending. Only Choice (B) gives the proper adverb "schnell" without an ending.

12. (C)

This question asks you to select the correct modifying adjective to correspond to the noun "Armen." Choice (B) offers the Infinitive of the verb "brechen," and Choice (D) the 3rd Person Singular Present Tense. Both forms can never be used as adjectives, and should not be considered. Choice (A) is the Present Participle ("breaking") used as an adjective, and Choice (C) a Past Participle ("broken"). However, only Choice (C) has the correct ending (-en) for an unpreceded adjective in the Dative Plural, and is therefore the right choice.

13. (A)

You are requested to find the proper verb completion for a sentence, in which the conjugated verb is a Modal Auxiliary verb (i.e. "müssen," "sollen," "können"). A sentence can only contain one conjugated verbform (here: "kann"). Therefore, Choices (B) and (C) have to be eliminated, since both are conjugated forms. (Choice (B) is the Present Tense, and Choice (C) the Simple Past.) In order to determine whether to use Choice (A) or Choice (B), you have to know that the proper verb compliment for a Modal is the Infinitive without "zu." The Infinitive with "zu" would have to be used if the conjugated verb would be a full verb, and not a Modal Auxiliary Verb.

14. (D)

You are requested to insert the proper relative pronoun to complete this sentence. If a relative pronoun is the object of a preposition, it has to be in the case which this preposition requires. "Aus" requires the dative. Choice (A) can only be a Nominative or an Accusative relative pronoun, and is therefore not possible. Choice (B) is an interrogative pronoun, which can never be used as a relative pronoun. Choice (C) is the Feminine Dative relative pronoun, and Choice (D) the Masculine and Neuter relative pronoun. The gender of a relative pronoun is determined by the word it refers back to (here: "Glas"), which is Neuter. The correct Choice is (D).

15. (B)

The task is to determine the Auxiliary verb that would fit with the Infinitive "kommen" and with the Subject "Dieter." Furthermore, the time expression "Morgen" indicates that the whole sentence is in the Future Tense. The Subject "Dieter" is Singular, which makes Choice (A) incorrect, because "werden" is Plural. Choice (C) is the Simple Past form of "werden," and is only used when "werden" is a full verb ("to become") and in the Passive Voice, which would require the Past Participle of "kommen" at the end of the sentence ("gekommen"). Choice (D) offers the Past Participle of "werden," which cannot be the conjugated part of the verb. The correct answer is Choice (B), in which the 3rd Person Singular form of "werden" is used as the auxiliary for the Future Tense.

16. (C)

You have to identify the correct form of the verb "empfehlen." In order to do so, you have to be familiar with all forms of this particular verb. "Empfehlen" has, as many verbs, a vowel change in the Present Tense. Vowel changes take effect only in the 2nd and 3rd Persons Singular. Choice (A) is incorrect, since the vowel is not changed.

Furthermore, you have to know that all verbs with a vowel change in the Present Tense are strong (n-) verbs, which means that they again change their vowel in the Simple Past. Therefore, Choice (B) is impossible, since it offers the Simple Past of a weak (t-) verb. Choice (D) does not correspond with the Subject ("der Ober") and is also wrong. The correct Choice is (C).

17. (A)

This question deals with the proper use of indefinite pronouns (i.e. "no one, someone, everyone"). Indefinite pronouns in German behave like unpreceded adjectives: they take the ending of the definite article, if it was used, with the exception of the Nominative, when they do not take any ending. In order to find the correct answer, you have to determine whether the indefinite pronoun is the Subject, the Accusative Object, or the Dative Object. Since the sentence only contains a verb ("klatschte"), a prepositional phrase ("in der Loge"), and an adverb ("begeistert"), the missing element must be the Subject. Choice (B) offers the Dative ending, Choice (C) the Accusative ending, and Choice (D) the Genitive ending. The correct answer is Choice (A).

18. (A)

The verb form "gestohlen worden" indicates that this sentence is in the Passive Voice, which means the subject of the sentence is acted upon and not acting itself. The second element "worden" shows that the tense of the sentence is either Present or Past Perfect. Although the verb "stehlen" takes "haben" as its auxiliary verb (Choice (D)), the auxiliary verb for Passive Perfect Tenses is always "sein." Choice (B) is wrong, because a form of "werden" is used as the auxiliary verb in the Passive Voice only in the Present, Simple Past, and Future Tenses. In a Passive sentence, the thing or the person acting is not the subject of the sentence, but a prepositional phrase ("von den Einbrechern"). The subject of this sentence is "das Geld," which is Singular. Therefore, Choice (C) is incorrect, and Choice (A) is the correct answer.

19. (D)

This question requires that you know the proper use of the preposition "wegen," and that you know the gender of the noun "Regen." "Wegen" is one of the few German prepositions which take the Genitive (the other ones are "trotz," "während," and "anstatt"). Only choices (B) and (D) are Genitive forms of the definite article. Therefore, Choices (A) and (C) are incorrect. Choice (B), however, is the Feminine form of the definite article, and since "Regen" is Masculine, the correct answer is Choice (D) "des."

20. (D)

In order to find the correct answer to this question, you have to know that the Superlative form of an Adjective is required to complete this sentence. All Choices are forms of the adjective "hoch," except Choice (C), which is the Superlative of "hoch" as an Adverb. Choice (A) is a Comparative form and consequently incorrect. Choice (B) offers a Positive form of "hoch" and is also wrong. The correct answer is Choice (D).

21. (D)

You are asked to find the proper preposition to complete this sentence. The Tense of the sentence is the Present Tense. German uses the Present Tense with a prepositional phrase in the Dative to express an activity that began in the past and is continuing in the present (i.e. "He has been living here for two years"). Choice (A) is wrong, because the preposition "vor" is used to indicate an event which happened in the past and is *not* continuing ("20 years ago"). "Nach" (Choice (B)) would be used in order to express the equivalent of the English phrase "after 20 years." Choice (D) would be a literal translation of the intended meaning ("for 20 years"). The correct answer is Choice (D).

22. (B)

The question deals with the German verb "gefallen," which is used in order to express that someone likes something. The thing or the person who is liked is the subject of the sentence, and the person who likes that thing or that person is a Dative object of "gefallen." In the example the Dative Object is missing. There is no noun-phrase offered as a possible choice, therefore, the missing element must be a Personal Pronoun. Choices (A) and (D), however, are Possessive Pronouns, which are very similar to Personal Pronouns, but they have a different function in a sentence. Choice (B) "mir" and Choice (C) "mich" are both Personal Pronouns (First Person Singular), but "mich" is the Accusative form. The correct Choice is (B).

23. (A)

The task is to find the proper preposition to complement the verb "warten." The English phrase "to wait for" is translated into German as "warten auf." Furthermore, German uses a "da-compound," if the Object of a Preposition is a Pronoun, *and* the Pronoun replaces a thing or an idea, and not a person. Therefore, Choices (B) (Preposition and Personal Pronoun), and (D) ("wo-compound") are wrong. Choice (C) is incorrect, since it offers the "da-compound" of the wrong preposition ("da") for the verb "fahren." The only possible Choice is (A).

24. (A)

You are asked to select the proper preposition to complete this sentence. The two German conjunctions, "wenn" and "als," and the Interrogative Pronoun, "wann," mean "when" in English. "Als" is used if the sentence is referring to a single event in the past, "wann" for an indirect question of time, and "wenn" covers all other instances. The conjunction "ob" also means "if" in English, but only when it is used in the sense of "whether" (indirect yes/no-question). Since this sentence refers to a single event in the past, and is not an indirect question, the correct Choice is (A).

25. (C)

You are asked to find the logical completion for the time Adverb "immer." German uses "immer" and a comparative of an adverb for something that becomes stronger and stronger. Choice (A) gives the Superlative form of the Adverb "lang," and may not be used. Choice (B) is the Positive Form of the Adverb and, therefore, also improper. Choice (D) ("mehr lang") is a construction, which German does not have, but English uses for the Comparative of Adverbs of more than two syllables (i.e. "more beautiful"). The correct Choice is (C).

26. (C)

German uses certain Adverbs in order to express doubt, anger, surprise, or delight. The proper use of these Adverbs, or "gesture-words," is very idiomatic, and requires a lot of practice. The sentence here expresses that the speaker is very upset about something, and wishes that the event had not occurred. ("My god, that cannot be true.") The only Adverb that is idiomatically correct, and emphasizes his anger, is "doch" (Choice (C)).

27. (A)

You have to find the correct coordinating conjunction to complete the sentence. It has to be a coordinating conjunction, since the verb in the second clause is in 2nd position. Choice (B) "weil" is a subordinating conjunction, which would require that the verb goes to the end of the clause. Choice (D) means "then," and must not be confused with the coordinated conjunction "denn." Choices (A) and (C) both mean "but," however, "sondern" is only used if the first clause is a negative clause, and the 2nd clause implies "but on the contrary." Since both these conditions are fulfilled, Choice (A) is correct.

28. (C)

You have to determine the proper verb form. Choice (B) "verstehe" is incorrect, because in German you can understand a sentence or a book, but not a country. Choice (D) "mag" is also improper, since the adverbial construction "sehr gut" ("very well") does not make sense with "mag." (You can like a country "very much," but not "very well.") The German verbs "wissen" and "kennen" both mean "to know," but "wissen" means "to know a fact," whereas "kennen" means "to be acquainted with." It is possible to be acquainted with a country, but not to know a country as a fact. Choice (C) is the correct answer.

29. (C)

This question examines your mastery of vocabulary. You have to know that "to make a decision" means "eine Entscheidung treffen" (Choice (C)). All Choices offered have something to do with an act you could perform after a long deliberation ("Nach langem Nachdenken"), but only "Entscheidung" can be used with the verb "treffen," of which "getroffen" is the Past Participle.

30. (A)

This question tests whether you can use the Reflexive verb "sich erkälten" ("to catch a cold") properly. A Reflexive verb is a verb that always needs a Reflexive Pronoun to be complete. In sentences with a Reflexive Pronoun, the Subject and the Object of the sentence are identical. The Subject of the sentence here is "man," an impersonal Pronoun. Therefore, you have to choose the 3rd Person Singular Reflexive Pronoun "sich."

31. (A)

This question tests your mastery of vocabulary. In order to answer correctly, you have to know that you cannot translate the English phrase "to be interested in" literally into German (Choice (C)). Choices (B) and (D) are also idiomatically improper. The correct Choice is (A).

32. (D)

In order to determine the correct answer you have to know what the phrase "above all" means in German. All choices come close to the intended meaning, but only Choice (D) can be used with the preposition "vor" and the noun "Dingen." Choice (A) "jeden" is idiomatically used as "In jedem Fall" ("in any case"), Choice (B) as "Beim ersten Mal" ("at the first time"), and Choice (C) as "In keinem Fall" ("under no circumstances").

33. (A)

This question again examines your mastery of vocabulary. You have to know that "Denkmal" means "Monument," and that "errichten" means "to erect." If you know these two words, which are frequently used combined, you arrive at the correct answer by determining that monuments are usually not "read" (Choice (B)), "bought" (Choice (C)), or "found" (Choice (D)).

34. (B)

All four possible Choices have something to do with what could happen if someone wants to buy a new house. In order to come to the correct conclusion, you have to realize that the first clause is in the Subjunctive. It indicates that your parents would like to have a new house, but are, for some reason, unable to get one. The only choice which would logically conclude the sentence is Choice (B). You have to know that "sich etwas leisten können" means "to be able to afford something."

35. (B)

The meaning of this sentence is that Jürgen, since he is only a little child, is always expected to do something with his mouth. You have to know that the phrase "den Mund halten" means "to shut up" or "to be quiet." If you know that, you arrive at the conclusion that only Choice (C) "halten" is a logically meaningful completion, which expresses something that Jürgen is supposed to do *because* he is a little child.

36. (B)

This question deals with the idiomatic use of the verb "lassen" ("to let"). As in English, this verb is sometimes used as a Modal Auxiliary verb, which means that it modifies the meaning of the main verb. In this sentence here the main verb is "waschen." If "lassen" is used in combination with "können," it expresses that the speaker wants someone else to initiate the activity expressed in the main verb, but not to perform it himself. Choices (A), (C), and (D) offer Modal Auxiliary verbs, which cannot be used with another Modal. The only possible Choice is (B).

37. (D)

In order to determine the correct answer, you have to know the meaning of the two German conjunctions "Je... desto," which are always used combined. They correspond to the English "The ... the" as in "the more he practices, the more he learns." You can eliminate Choices (A) and (B) immediately, because this sentence requires a conjunction, and neither "trotz" nor "um zu" are conjunctions. Choice (C) "aber" is a conjunction; however, it does not complete a sentence whose first clause starts with "Je."

38. (C)

This question requires that you know which idiomatic phrase German uses in order to express that someone's watch or clock is fast. Although all four Choices present verbs that have something to do with movement, only choice (C) "vorgeht" is correct in this context.

39. (A)

This question asks you to identify a construction that German very often employs to express a hypothetical situation. Above all, you have to see that this sentence is in the Subjunctive Mood, and that the first clause is a "Wenn-clause," which means that the second clause is the main clause of the whole sentence. This conclusion eliminates Choices (B), an interrogative Pronoun, and (C), a coordinating conjunction. Choice (D) is logically impossible. The correct Choice is (A).

40. (C)

The most important thing you have to know to determine the correct answer is the meaning of the conjunction "obwohl" ("although"). In this sentence this conjunction indicates that parents love their children, although they do something parents do not like. Choices (A), (B), and (D) describe something positive, and they would only make sense if the conjunctions "weil" ("because"), or "wenn" ("if," "when") were used. The correct and logical answer is Choice (C).

41. (C)

In question 41 you are asked to find the logical verb completion for "ist" as the auxiliary verb. A form of the verb "sein" is often used as the auxiliary verb for the Present Perfect Tense. The only possible form for the main verb is a Past Participle. (Past Participles usually have a ge-Prefix, and can easily be recognized, i.e. "gefahren," "gekommen.") Choice (A) offers an Infinitive, and not a Past Participle, which would only make sense if the auxiliary verb was "wird" (Future Tense) or a Modal Verb (i.e. "sollen," "können"). Choice (D) gives the Simple Past of the verb "fahren." The only two Past Participles offered are "geantwortet" (Choice (B)), and "geblieben" (Choice (C)). However, "antworten" takes "haben" as its auxiliary verb for the Present Perfect. The correct answer is Choice (C).

42. (A)

Question 42 asks you to find the correct Accusative object to complement the verb "hatte." You have to know that "haben" is a verb that requires an Accusative Object. The adjective ending "-e" added to "kein" can only be Accusative Feminine Singular (i.e. "keine Frau"), or Accusative Plural (i.e. "keine Kinder"). Choice (B) "Hunger" is Masculine, and Choice (C) "Bier" is Neuter. Choice (D) "Uhr" is idiomatically awkward, since this noun refers only to the object telling the time (watch or clock; i.e. "Ich habe eine neue Uhr") and not to a time span. The correct choice is (A).

43. (C)

Choice (A) is the best answer for this question. You are asked which preposition would complete this sentence. Many German conjunctions have a basic meaning, and a second meaning, when they are used in time expressions. Two of these conjunctions are "während" and "in." "Zu" and "auf" are not used in time expressions and can therefore never be used with the noun "Sommer" ("summer"). The preposition "während," however, would require that "Sommer" were preceded by a definite article. You can conclude that the only possible answer is Choice (C).

44. (D)

In order to determine the proper answer for this question you have to connect this sentence with sentence 43. Sentence 43 states that someone goes to the sea every summer. The definite pronoun "das" at the beginning of sentence 44 refers back to the previous clause, and it expresses that the fact that someone goes to the sea every summer is nice for the children. The most appropriate completion is Choice (D) "besonders." Choices (A) – (C) are grammatically possible, but would not make much sense.

45. (B)

This sentence gives the cause for the fact indicated in sentence 44; in other words, it tells you by using the coordinating conjunction "denn" why it is especially nice for the children to go to the sea. The Infinitive at the end of the clause tells you that the reason is that the children play at the beach. You are asked to find the proper Modal auxiliary verb to compliment the Infinitive "spielen" ("to play"). If you put the sentence in context with sentences 43 and 44, only Choice (B), which indicates that the children *can* play at the beach, provides a sensible completion.

46. (C)

You are asked to find the most meaningful and grammatically correct adjective that modifies the noun "Fussballspieler" ("soccer-player"). Choices (A) and (D) are both grammatically incorrect and not meaningful in connection with this noun. Choices (B) and (C) are both meaningful options, but since "Fussballspieler" is Masculine and its function is a Predicate Noun, only Choice (C) "berühmter" carries the proper strong Adjective-ending.

47. (A)

You are requested to find the Proper Personal pronoun to complete this sentence. Again, you have to connect this sentence with the previous one. It is clear that the Pronoun you have to insert refers back to Franz Beckenbauer. Since he is male, you have to find the Masculine Accusative Singular Personal Pronoun, which is "ihn." Consequently, Choice (A) is the correct answer.

48. (C)

This sentence contains two Personal Pronouns which refer back to sentences 46 and 47. "Sie" refers back to "viele Leute" in sentence 47 and "ihn" to "Franz Beckenbauer" in sentence 46. Sentence 46 says that Beckenbauer was a famous soccer-player, and sentence 47 expresses that people still talk about him. If you consider this information, only Choice (C) "vergessen" ("to forget") is a logical completion for this sentence.

49. (A)

The most important thing you have to know in order to answer this question is that the phrase "to make a decision" means "einen Entschluss fassen." Furthermore, you have to recognize that the sentence is in the Present Perfect, and therefore the missing element is a Past Participle. All Choices have something to do with what a person can do with his senses, but only Choice (A) is used with the Direct Object "Entschluss."

50. (C)

You have to realize that the phrase following the main clause is not a complete clause, since there is no element which could be the Subject of this clause. Therefore, the missing element must be an Infinitive with "zu," on which the prepositional phrase "mit dem Rauchen" is depending. For that reason Choices (A) and (B) can be eliminated, since Choice (A) offers an Infinitive without "zu," and Choice (B) a Past Participle. In order to decide between Choices (C) and (D) you have to know that the verb "aufhören" is a separable prefix verb, and that this group of verbs inserts "zu" between the prefix and the main verb in an infinitive construction. The correct Choice is (C).

51. (B)

You have to know that the verb "leicht fallen" means that something is easy for someone, and that the person for whom it is easy is in the Dative. Since Choice (A) offers the Accusative lst Person Singular Personal Pronoun, Choice (C) the Nominative 1st Person Singular Personal Pronoun, and Choice (D) a Possessive Adjective which requires a Noun to complement it, the correct Choice is (B).

52. (D)

Above all, you have to know that the verb "lesen" takes "haben" as its Auxiliary Verb in the Present Perfect. Choice (C) is incorrect, because "werden" is the Auxiliary for the Future Tense, the adverb "gestern" refers to the Past, and because "lesen" would be in the Infinitive and not in the Past Participle. Since the Auxiliary has to be in agreement with the Subject of the clause ("ich"), Choice (D) is the correct answer.

53. (C)

All four Choices offer forms of the word "romantisch." However, if an Adjective follows a form of the Verb "sein," and if it is not modifying a noun, it is used as a Predicate Adjective. Predicate Adjectives do not take endings in German, and consequently Choice (C) is the correct answer to this question.

54. (C)

The clause does not have a verb which immediately eliminates Choice (A), because the coordinating Conjunction "denn" can only be used in complete clauses. Choice (B) "sondern" is wrong, since it means "but, on the contrary," and is only used if the preceding clause is a negative statement. In order to determine between Choices (C) and (D) you have to know that the Adverb "jedenfalls" means "at any rate," which would not make sense. The correct answer is Choice (C).

55. (D)

First of all, you have to know that the reflexive Verb "sich freuen" always takes "auf" plus Accusative (Choice (C)) as its prepositional complement. Choice (A) is a literal translation of the English equivalent "to look forward to," and would be inappropriate in German. The preposition "nach" (Choice (B)) is only used in time expression to indicate a specific time of day (i.e. "viertel nach eins").

56. (B)

The verb "versammeln" means in this context "to gather," and in German it is always used reflexively, when it has this particular meaning. Therefore, the missing element in this clause is the proper Reflexive Pronoun. You have to know that a Reflexive Pronoun is used when the Subject and the Object of a sentence are identical. Here, the Subject is "die ganze Familie," which is Feminine Singular. The correct Feminine 3rd Person Feminine Singular Reflexive Pronoun is "sich" (Choice (B)).

57. (D)

In order to arrive at the correct answer, you must realize that the whole clause (Questions 55-57) is in the Present Tense, since the Adverb "immer" in clause 55 indicates that everything which is said is referring to a recurring event. Therefore, you have to choose the proper Present Tense form of the Modal Verb "können," which is Choice (D).

58. (C)

This question deals with different adverbs indicating quantities. To arrive at the correct answer you have to know that "more... than" means "mehr ... als." Choice (A) ("am meisten") is the superlative Adverb "the most;" Choice (B) ("viel") means in this context "a lot;" Choice (D) ("meistens") is a time expression meaning "mostly." The correct answer is Choice (C) ("mehr"), which is the Comparative of "viel" and the only of the offered Choices which can idiomatically be used with "als."

59. (B)

This question asks you to find the correct Adjective ending for "viel," when it modifies the noun "Überstunden." First of all, you have to realize that "Überstunden" is in the Plural. "Viel" only takes on endings when it modifies a Noun in the Plural, and it is unpreceded when it modifies a Noun in the Singular (Choice (A)). In order to determine which of the three remaining Choices offers the correct ending, you have to realize that "Überstunden" is the direct Object of the sentence. Therefore, you have to choose the Accusative Plural ending, which is -e. The correct answer is Choice (B).

60. (D)

You have to insert the proper Relative Pronoun to complete this sentence. Usually, the number and the gender of a German Relative Pronoun are determined by its antecedent, and its case is determined by its function in the Relative clause. The only exceptions to this rule are if the antecedent is unknown, or if the whole main clause is the antecedent. The latter is the case in this sentence. The Relative clause does not refer back to "Überstunden," but to the whole clause. Therefore, the Relative Pronoun "was" (Choice (D)) has to be used. The Relative Pronouns "das" and "die" (Choices (A) and (C)) are only used when the antecedent is known, and "wie" (Choice (B)) can never be used as a Relative Pronoun.

61. (B)

Question 61 asks you to identify the attitude of the author towards his text. In order to come to the correct conclusion, you have to understand that the author tries to summarize Bismarck's achievements (Choice (B)). He does not give his own evaluation of these achievements, nor does he assess Bismarck's politics. You must recognize that the author only wants to give a brief overview of Bismarck's domestic and foreign policies, without mentioning whether one or the other was more important to him (Choice (A)) without passing a value judgement on Bismarck's ideas (Choice (C)); and without making an assumption about his overall significance for the German history (Choice (D)). He merely quotes other people who have said that Bismarck was "one of the most important figures in German history."

62. (D)

Question 62 wants you to deduce one of Bismarck's characteristics. In order to come to the logical conclusion you have to collect carefully the information provided in the text. Choice (A) should immediately be dismissed, since the text states that Bismarck saw Socialism as a danger, and for that reason it is safe to say that he definitely was not a Socialist and did not want a revolution (Choice (C)). Choice (B) is wrong, because the Past Participle "entschieden" means "decided," and the text does not mention the outcome of the "Kulturkampf," but only that it was a severe problem for Bismarck. The correct answer is Choice (D), because the text does say that Bismarck saw parliaments as something "evil," and it is correct to derive that he did not like them.

63. (B)

This question tests your comprehension of a specific sentence of the text. In order to answer correctly (Choice (B)), you have to understand that the first sentence of the last paragraph says that Bismarck's major accomplishment in foreign politics was that he established Germany beside France, England and Russia as a superpower in Europe. The only Choice which expresses the equivalent to this statement is Choice (B). The terms used for the other Choices are mentioned in the text, but not in connection with Bismarck's foreign policies.

64. (C)

Question 64 asks you to evaluate the relationship of Thomas and Heinrich Mann based on the information provided in the text. It is obvious that they did not love each other very much (Choice (B)), and the text does not mention that they ever wrote anything together (Choice (D)). Choice (A) claims that the brothers always argued. The text, however, states that their relationship was a problematic one, but that they had a reconciliation after their return from the United States after the end of World War II. If you consider all the information you have, only Choice (C) is fully supported by the text.

65. (C)

This question tests whether you have understood a certain paragraph of the text. You have to comprehend what the brothers did between 1933 and 1945. The text says that Thomas and Heinrich had to emigrate to the United States due to Hitler's rise to power. Since German uses the terms "USA" and "Amerika" often synonymously, Choice (C) is the correct answer. The other countries (France, the DDR, Switzerland) are mentioned somewhere in the text, but not in the context of the time period between 1933 and 1945.

66. (C)

Question 66 asks you to make a general assumption about Heinrich Mann's life. Choice (A) claims that it was typical for a "Zivilisationslit-erat," which cannot be derived from the text, because all that is said about a "Zivilisationsliterat" is that Thomas used this term to describe his brother. Choice (B) offers a comparison between the fact that Heinrich was at one time a Presidential candidate, and the lives of Presidential candidates in general. This assertion is not supported by the text, either. The contention of Choice (D) that Heinrich's life was characterized by the fall of the German Empire in 1918 can also not be verified with the text, since it only mentions Thomas' reluctance to embrace the Republic after the fall of the Empire. Choice (C), which says that Thomas' and Heinrich's lives were very closely connected, is the only logical answer.

67. (B)

This question attempts to compare the political convictions of Thomas and Heinrich Mann. Throughout the text it becomes clear that the friction between the brothers was partially caused by different political views. Therefore, they cannot have been either similar ("ähnlich," Choice (A)) or identical ("gleich," Choice (C)). Choice (D) ("reaktionär," "reactionary") also finds no support in the text, since only Thomas' political views were at a certain point in his life reactionary. The correct Choice is (B), which says that their views were different ("unterschiedlich").

68. (A)

In this question you have to make an inference based on statements made in the text. The correct answer is Choice (A). Nowhere in the text is it directly said that TV sets cause fires, but it is obvious from the context that some fires are caused by TV sets. For any of the statements made in Choices (B) – (D) no proof can be found in the text.

69. (A)

In order to answer this question correctly you have to understand how the judge substantiates his decision in this case. He reasons that TV sets today have such a high standard that they do not need to be watched all the time. Therefore, Choice (A) is the correct answer. Choice (C) runs counter to all the facts given in the article; the statement of Choice (B) is not mentioned in the text; and Choice (B), which says that miraculously TV shows become worse and worse, could only be considered when you completely misunderstand the content of Choice (D).

70. (B)

To answer this question you have to comprehend what statement the judge makes when he refers to the quality of TV shows. He says that it is not surprising that due to the quality of TV shows people fall asleep, and in this context it is clear that he means due to their bad quality. The correct Choice is (B), which infers that TV shows are boring ("langweilig"), and consequently people fall asleep and cannot be held responsible.

71. (B)

This question asks you to assess what the tenants association does. It neither states that the owner of the TV set is responsible for the fire (Choice (A)), nor does it claim that nobody is allowed to fall asleep in front of his TV set (Choice (C)), nor does it criticize the judge's decision (Choice (D)). The tenants association only objectively reports what has happened in this particular case (Choice (B)).

72. (B)

Question 72 tests your comprehension of what the landlord's intentions were for suing his tenant. Choice (B) is the correct answer. In order to come to that conclusion you have to know that "seine Verluste erstattet bekommen" means "to get reimbursed for one's losses," which is precisely what the landlord wants to accomplish. He does not necessarily want a new insurance policy (Choice (A)), although he might consider it, nor is he suing the tenants association's newspaper (Choice (D)), nor does he want a new TV set (Choice (C)).

73. (D)

You have to understand what the findings of the investigation were which the doctors at the hospital in Münster conducted. The text says the results were that there exists the possibility that already before the year 2000 more women than men will die of heart attacks, lung cancer, and carcinomas. The doctors support their assumption with the increasing numbers of women dying of these illnesses, which is stated in Choice (D). It is essential to know that the German verb "zunehmen" means "to increase." Choice (A) is incorrect, because the text does not suggest that "men-diseases" should from now on be called "women-diseases." Choice (B) is wrong, since the absolute number of men dying of heart attacks today is still larger than the number of women passing away for the same reason. Choice (C) should not be considered because the adverb "kaum" means "hardly," and the text does not say that in the year 2000 women will hardly die of heart attacks.

74. (B)

In order to make the right choice you have to fully comprehend the meaning of the direct quote in the second paragraph. You have to know that "aufholen" means "to catch up," and that "immer mehr" means "more and more." Consequently, Dr. Dittrich says that women are catching up in every respect, and that more and more young women are coming to the hospital with typical "male" diseases. The only choice which partially concurs with this statement is Choice (B).

75. (B)

You are asked to identify one possible reason for the development that women suffer more and more heart attacks. Since the doctors who conducted the study are uncertain about it, some psychologists contend that one of the reasons is that women as a result of emancipation want to lead a "male" life, and that as a consequence women also acquire "male" diseases. The correct Choice is (B). Choice (A) offers one of the effects (and not one of the causes) of the development under consideration, namely that life expectancy of women will decrease, and Choices (C) and (D) would misrepresent the statements made in the text.

76. (A)

In order to arrive at the correct solution to this question, you have to realize that it becomes evident throughout the text that the doctors are more than anything baffled by the fact that the number of women dying of "male" diseases is increasing, and that they have no positive explanation to offer. Therefore, Choice (A) "bemerkenswert" ("astonishing") is the correct answer.

77. (C)

Question 77 wants you to make the proper conclusion why the incidents described in the text are newsworthy. Choice (A) says that it is common practice for a considerable amount of time to duplicate counterfeit money with a color copier, a statement which is not made in the text. Choices (B) and (D), namely that it is impossible to reproduce bogus money with a color copier (B), and that it is now legal in the state of Hessen to copy money with that particular device (D), would certainly be newsworthy if they were true, but they are not supported by the text. The correct answer is Choice (C).

78. (A)

The task of this question is to determine which role the license plate of the car plays in the story. The correct answer is Choice (A). You have to understand that the cashier of the store where the woman tried to buy stockings did not initially suspect that anything was wrong with the bill. After awhile she became suspicious, ran out of the store, and was able to write down the license plate number. Choices (B) - (D) all refer to something that happened with the counterfeit money, and not with the plate.

79. (B)

This question also deals with the second paragraph in which the events that took place in the store are described. You are asked to evaluate what the cashier did. Obviously she did not fabricate the counterfeit money (Choice (A)), but helped to catch a criminal. She neither immediately ("sofort") realized that something was wrong with the bill (Choice (B)), nor personally lead the police to the apartment of the woman's friend (Choice (D)). The correct answer is Choice (B), which says that she alertly ("geistesgegenwärtig") did the right thing, after she became suspicious.

80. (D)

In order to answer this question correctly you have to understand the last paragraph. This paragraph puts the whole story into a broader context by stating that the police as of now do not know whether the couple alone had the idea to copy the money with the help of a color copier, or whether other criminals use the same method. Since the police have already determined who the woman is (Choice (A)), how the money was fabricated (Choice (B)), and whether the 500-Mark bill was genuine or not (Choice (C)), the correct answer is Choice (D).

GERMAN TEST VI

PART A

Time: 1 Hour
80 Questions

DIRECTIONS: Each of the sentences in this part has a blank space indicating that a word or phrase has been omitted. From the four choices select the ONE that when inserted in the sentence fits grammatically and logically with the sentence as a whole. Then blacken the corresponding space on the answer sheet.

1. Ich bin ihm zufällig auf der Straße ... .

(A) begegnet
(B) getroffen
(C) kennengelernt
(D) entgegengegangen

2. Das Land hat Schulden in Höhe von DM 1 000 000 000, also eine ... Mark.

(A) Million
(B) Milliarde
(C) Billion
(D) Trillion

3. Der Satz "Das hätte ich machen können" besteht aus fünf ... .

(A) Worten
(B) Wörten
(C) Wortern
(D) Wörtern

4. Die Stadt Konstanz in Süddeutschland liegt .... .

(A) an der Bodensee
(B) am Bodensee
(C) auf der Bodensee
(D) an den Bodensee

5. In diesem Semester habe ich an der Universität fünf ... belegt.

(A) Klassen
(B) Stunden
(D) Kurse
(D) Stände

6. Gestern abend haben wir drei Stunden lang Deutsch .... .

(A) studiert
(B) gelernt
(C) gestudiert
(D) studieren

7. Meine Schwester weiß es schon lange, aber ich habe es ... heute gehört.

(A) nur
(B) allein
(C) erst
(D) einzig

8. Jeden Abend sendet das erste Programm .... .

(A) die Neuen
(B) die Neuigkeiten
(C) die Nachrichten
(D) das Neue

9. Was halten Sie vom neuen Präsidenten? Ich ....

(A) halte ihn intelligent
(B) halte von ihm intelligent
(C) halte ihm für intelligent
(D) halte ihn für intelligent

10. Wir ... uns ein neues Haus bauen.

(A) lassen
(B) machen
(C) haben
(D) gehen

11. Sie sagte, sie würde das machen, und ....

(A) es ist ihr gelungen
(B) sie hat gelungen
(C) sie ist gelungen
(D) es hat ihr gelungen

12. Das ist mein Privatzimmer. Du ... nicht in das Zimmer hineingehen!

(A) mußt
(B) darfst
(C) magst
(D) kannst

13. "Guten Abend, Herr Generaldirektor. Dürfte ich Ihnen meine Frau ... ?" "Ich freue mich, Ihre Bekanntschaft zu machen, gnädige Frau."

(A) einführen
(B) einleiten
(C) vorstellen
(D) einbringen

14. Ich … nicht, wie die Frau heißt.

(A) kenne
(B) kann
(C) weiß
(D) wisse

15. Er hat seine Frau und seine Kinder … und ist nach Australien gegangen.

(A) abgefahren
(B) liegenlassen
(C) hinterlassen
(D) verlassen

16. Ich … , es wird bald regnen.

(A) denke daran
(B) halte
(C) glaube
(D) danke

17. Das ist ein interessantes Ehepaar; die Frau ist Amerikanerin und der … ist Japaner.

(A) man
(B) Mann
(C) Mensch
(D) Man

18. Mein Vater trinkt gern Bier, aber noch … trinkt er Wein.

(A) lieber
(B) gerner
(C) vielmehr
(D) sondern

19. "Dürfte ich Herrn Schmidt sprechen, bitte?" "Hier gibt es keinen Schmidt. Welche ... haben Sie gewählt?"

(A) Zahl
(B) Anzahl
(C) Ziffer
(D) Nummer

20. Herr Ober, ich habe vor einer halben Stunde eine Bratwurst .... Wie lange muß ich noch warten?

(A) bestellt
(B) befohlen
(C) geordnet
(D) verlangt

PART B

DIRECTIONS: The sentences below contain blank spaces indicating omissions in the text. Below each blank are four choices. Select the choice that is grammatically correct in the context and blacken the corresponding space on the answer sheet. Be sure to read the sentences first.

21. Ich gehe heute in die Stadt, ...

(A) weil ich einkaufen muß
(B) denn ich einkaufen muß
(C) weil ich muß einkaufen
(D) damit ich einkaufen muß

22. ... , und fühle mich jetzt hier zu Hause.

(A) Ich habe seit drei Jahren in Berlin gewohnt
(B) Ich habe für drei Jahre in Berlin gewohnt
(C) Ich wohne für drei Jahre in Berlin
(D) Ich wohne seit drei Jahren in Berlin

23. Ich habe ... geschenkt.

(A) eine Uhr dem Mann
(B) dem Mann eine Uhr
(C) die Uhr ihm
(D) dem Mann sie

24. Unser Lehrer ... .

(A) will uns fleißig zu arbeiten
(B) will uns fleißig arbeiten
(C) will, daß wir fleißig arbeiten
(D) will, daß wir arbeiten fleißig

25. Weil ich kein Geld hatte, habe ich ... .

(A) arbeiten gemußt
(B) gearbeitet müssen
(C) arbeiten müssen
(D) müssen arbeiten

26. Das Buch ... auf dem Tisch.

(A) legte
(B) liegte
(C) lag
(D) lagte

27. Maria, ... den Schulaufsatz schon geschrieben?

(A) haben Sie
(B) habt ihr
(C) hast du
(D) habst du

28. ... ins Kino.

(A) Nach dem Essen wir gehen
(B) Nach dem Essen gehen wir
(C) Wir nach dem Essen gehen
(D) Gehen nach dem Essen wir

29. Wenn es morgen … , arbeiten wir nicht.

(A) regnen würde
(B) regnete
(C) regnet
(D) geregnet hätte

30. Wenn ich mehr Geld … , hätte ich einen Urlaub machen können.

(A) verdient hätte
(B) verdient habe
(C) verdiene
(D) verdienen würde

31. Meine Schwester sagte, sie … keinen Kuchen mehr, aber ich glaube ihr nicht.

(A) hatte
(B) habe
(C) hat
(D) wäre

32. Die Kinder sind immer … zur Schule gegangen.

(A) während der Tag
(B) während des Tages
(C) während dem Tag
(D) während den Tag

33. Ich warte … .

(A) auf dich zu kommen
(B) für dich zu kommen
(C) darauf, daß du kommst
(D) auf daß du kommst

34. Sie ist gestern nach Hause gefahren, ...

(A) ohne besuchend mich
(B) ohne mich besuchen
(C) ohne mich zu besuchen
(D) ohne sie mich besucht hat

35. Ich arbeite, um mir ein Auto zu kaufen, aber mein Vater hat gearbeitet, ...

(A) damit seine Kinder studieren könnten
(B) um seine Kinder zu studieren
(C) um seine Kinder studieren könnten
(D) damit seine Kinder zu studieren

36. Es gibt hier ... , die das verstehen können.

(A) keinen Studenten
(B) keine Studenten
(C) kein Student
(D) kein Studenten

37. Er hat die Polizei angerufen, und sie ... sofort gekommen.

(A) ist
(B) sind
(C) hat
(D) haben

38. Meine Freunde ... klassische Musik.

(A) sind interessiert in
(B) interessieren sich in
(C) interessieren sich für
(D) interessieren sich an

39. Haben Sie den neuen Tenor ... ?

(A) hören singen
(B) singen gehört
(C) gesungen hören
(D) singen hören

40. ... älter ich werde, ... langsamer ich arbeite.

(A) Das mehr – – das mehr
(B) So – – so
(C) Je – – desto
(D) Desto – – je

PART C

DIRECTIONS: The sentences below contain blank spaces indicating omissions in the text. Below each blank are four choices. Select the choice that is grammatically correct in the context and blacken the corresponding space on the answer sheet. Be sure to read the sentences first.

41. ... ich meine Großmutter besuchte, gab sie mir immer Kuchen.

(A) Als
(B) Wenn
(C) Wann
(D) Wahrend

Gibt es ... Wein mehr? ... , er steht ... Tisch.

42. (A) kein
(B) keinen
(C) nicht
(D) keiner

43. (A) Ja
(B) Nein
(C) Doch
(D) Nicht

44. (A) am
(B) an der
(C) auf dem
(D) auf den

Ihr Wagen ist alt, aber … ist neu. Er … mir letzte Woche von meinem Vater geschenkt.

45. (A) mein
(B) meiner
(C) meins
(D) meinen

46. (A) war
(B) wird
(C) wurde
(D) hat

Ich weiß, … er jetzt wohnt, aber ich weiß nicht, … seine Familie auch dort wohnt.

47. (A) wohin
(B) woher
(C) wo
(D) wer

48. (A) wenn
(B) ob
(C) weder
(D) Wetter

Der … Mann hat der … Frau geholfen.

49. (A) alter
(B) alte
(C) alten
(D) älter

50. (A) junger
(B) junge
(C) jungen
(D) jünger

51. … , der das Kind gerettet hatte, wurde von den Eltern

herzlich gedankt.

(A) Dem Studenten
(B) Dem Student
(C) Der Student
(D) Den Studenten

52. Mein Freund hat mir eine schöne Blume gegeben, ... mir sehr gefiel.

(A) der
(B) das
(C) was
(D) daß

53. Seine Familie wohnt in einem schönen Haus ... Schillerstraße.

(A) auf
(B) an der
(C) in
(D) in der

54. Ich habe ... die Frage nicht geantwortet.

(A) - - -
(B) auf
(C) zu
(D) an

55. Ich habe ... gewaschen.

(A) meine Hände
(B) mich die Hände
(C) mir den Händen
(D) mir die Hände

56.-57. Beethoven wurde ... ... geboren.

(A) 1770	in Bonn
(B) in 1770	in Bonn
(C) in Bonn	im Jahre 1770
(D) in Bonn	1770

58. Ich habe ihn ... noch einmal gesehen, aber er kannte mich nicht.

(A) einen Abend
(B) einem Abend
(C) eines Abends
(D) ein Abend

59. Das Wetter war schlecht, ... haben wir gearbeitet.

(A) aber
(B) aber trotzdem
(C) obwohl
(D) aber trotzdem gestern

60. Sie drehte ... um und schaute mich an.

(A) ---
(B) ihr
(C) sich
(D) langsam

PART D

DIRECTIONS: Read the following passages carefully for comprehension. Each passage is followed by a number of incomplete statements or questions. Select the completion or answer that is best according to the passage and blacken the corresponding space on the answer sheet.

Um 1300 hatten damalige Großstädte wie Wien, Hamburg, Nürnberg und Danzig über 20 000 Einwohner, und Köln hatte sogar nehezu

30 000. Venedig, Rom, und Paris waren noch größer. In den deutschen Städten erlebte der Kaufmannsstand im 14. Jahrhundert einen großen Aufstieg. Die Einwohner der Städte, die "Bürger," wurden immer reicher und traten deswegen mit dem Adel in Wettstreit, weil sie sich nicht nur wirtschaftlich, sondern auch politisch durchsetzen wollten. Manche Städte wurden von der Macht der Grafen und Herzöge befreit und durften sich selbst verwalten. Sie konnten sich direkt dem König unterstellen, und hießen daher "freie Städte." Hamburg und Bremen, die auch Mitglieder der Hansa waren, nennen sich noch heute stolz "freie Hansestädte."

61. In Deutschland gab es vor 1300

(A) keine großen Städte.
(B) mehrere große Städte.
(C) nur im Süden Großstädte.
(D) Städte mit mehr als 50 000 Einwohnern.

62. Die deutschen Städte im Spätmittelalter

(A) waren wirtschaftlich schwach.
(B) hatten kein Interesse an Politik.
(C) wollten vom Adel abhängig sein.
(D) wurden wirtschaftlich immer stärker.

63. Einige Städte hießen "freie Städte," weil sie

(A) Mitglieder der Hansa waren.
(B) von Grafen und Herzögen regiert wurden.
(C) nur dem König unterstellt waren.
(D) kein Geld zahlen mußten.

Vor dem zweiten Weltkrieg hatten fast alle Deutschen zwei Muttersprachen: das erst in der Schule erlernte Hochdeutsch und den zu Hause gesprochenen Dialekt. Manche Kinder glaubten sogar, eine Geheimsprache mit den Eltern zu haben, weil andere Hochdeutsch sprachen. Da die Bevölkerung ziemlich seßhaft war, blieben die

Dialekte verhältnismäßig rein. Nach 1945 kam es aber in Deutschland zu große Wanderungen. Viele Leute mußten ihre Heimat verlassen und in neue Gebiete übersiedeln. Diese Leute behielten ihre Dialekte, aber sie fanden häufig Ehepartner, die einen anderen Dialekt sprachen. Weil sie dann zu Hause keinen Dialekt sprechen konnten, wuchsen ihre Kinder ohne Dialekt auf. Deswegen gibt es heute in Deutschland viele Menschen, die keinen Dialekt sprechen können.

64. Vor dem zweiten Weltkrieg haben deutsche Kinder ihren Dialekt

(A) zu Hause gesprochen.
(B) nur in der Schule gesprochen.
(C) in der Schule gelernt.
(D) nicht mit den Eltern gesprochen.

65. Viele Ehepaare haben nach 1945 zu Hause keinen Dialekt gesprochen, weil

(A) sie keinen Dialekt konnten.
(B) sie eine Geheimsprache haben wollten.
(C) sie keinen Dialekt gemeinsam hatten.
(D) sie ihre Heimat vergessen wollten.

66. Viele Deutsche sprechen heute keinen Dialekt, weil

(A) ihre Eltern früh gestorben sind.
(B) ihre Eltern zu Hause keinen Dialekt gesprochen haben.
(C) sie in der Schule Hochdeutsch gelernt haben.
(D) sie als Kinder häufig übersiedelt sind.

In seinem Roman *Die Blechtrommel* erzählt Günter Grass die Geschichte von Oskar Matzerath, der vom Moment seiner Geburt an alles versteht, was um ihn vorgeht, und an seinem dritten Geburtstag beschließt, nicht weiter zu wachsen. Weil er dann nachher immer so aussieht, als wäre er erst drei Jahre alt, kann er ohne Bestrafung manches machen, was einem größeren Kind oder einem Erwachsenen nicht erlaubt wäre. Oskar hat zwei große Gaben: er kann mit seiner Stimme nicht nur Glas zerbrechen, sondern es auch kunstvoll schneiden; und er kann durch sein Trommeln die Gedanken und Gemüter der Menschen beeinflussen. In dieser grotesken Figur will Grass den Deutschen ihre eigenen Schwächen und Probleme vor Augen führen.

67. Oskar Matzerath ist

(A) ein normales Kind.
(B) ein sehr ungewöhnliches Kind.
(C) der Verfasser des Romans *Die Blechtrommel.*
(D) ein ungewöhnlich großes Kind.

68. Wenn Oskar etwas Unanständiges macht, wird er wegen seiner Größe

(A) immer erwischt und bestraft.
(B) von einem größerem Kind begleitet.
(C) nie gesehen.
(D) selten bestraft.

69. Oskar Matzerath kann

(A) mit den richtigen Werkzeugen kunstvoll Glas schneiden.
(B) durch Trommeln Glas zerbrechen.
(C) Menschen durch Trommeln verführen.
(D) Menschen durch seine Stimme stören.

70. Der Romanschriftsteller Günter Grass glaubt,

(A) die Deutschen haben weder Schwächen noch Probleme.
(B) die Literatur kann die Schwächen und Probleme eines Volkes verdeutlichen.
(C) die Deutschen sollten Oskar nachahmen.
(D) es wäre gut, wenn alle Deutschen Kinder bleiben würden.

Es ist fast dunkel, und das Auto rast schnell durch die Stadt. Ein Polizist, der sieht, wie gefährlich das sein könnte, hält es an. Er fragt den Fahrer: "Brennt es vielleicht irgendwo?" Der Fahrer sagt ganz höflich, "Nein." Weil er sieht, daß jemand neben dem Fahrer sitzt, fragt der Polizist weiter: "Fahren Sie so schnell, weil Sie Ihren Freund ins Krankenhaus bringen?" Noch einmal sagt der Fahrer "Nein," aber es ist klar, daß er ungeduldig wird. Da sagt der Polizist, "Wenn Sie keinen guten Grund dafür haben, sollten Sie eigentlich nicht so schnell durch die Stadt fahren, mein Herr." Darauf sagt der Fahrer: "Sehen Sie, Herr Wachtmeister, es wird jetzt dunkel. Ich will nach Hause kommen, bevor es ganz dunkel ist, weil meine Scheinwerfer kaputt sind. Und ich will nicht ohne Scheinwerfer fahren, weil meine Bremsen nicht funktionieren. Deswegen muß ich so schnell fahren. Gestatten Sie bitte, daß ich jetzt losfahre."

71. Der Polizist hält das Auto an, weil er glaubt,

(A) der Fahrer ist wahrscheinlich betrunken.
(B) es ist gefährlich, so durch die Stadt zu rasen.
(C) es muß irgendwo brennen.
(D) es wird bald dunkel sein.

72. Der Fahrer antwortet dem Polizisten höflich, aber er ist ungeduldig, weil

(A) der Polizist ihn beschimpft.
(B) er weiß, warum er bald zu Hause sein muß.
(C) er seinen Freund schnell ins Krankenhaus bringen will.
(D) er dem Polizisten nicht erklären will, warum er so schnell fährt.

73. Das Erstaunliche bei dieser Geschichte ist, daß

(A) der Fahrer nicht zu verstehen scheint, warum er nicht so schnell fahren sollte.
(B) der Polizist den Fahrer nicht beschimpft.
(C) der Fahrer so schnell fährt.
(D) der Passagier nichts zu sagen hat.

Erst mit der Veröffentlichung von Lavoisiers *Elemente der Chemie* im Jahre 1789 befreite sich die Chemie endgültig von der Herrschaft der Alchimie und wurde eine Naturwissenschaft im modernen Sinn, obwohl der Anfang der Chemie viel weiter zurückliegt. Für die Alchimisten waren die Naturwissenschaften Teile der Philosophie gewesen, aber Lavoisier befürwortete die Anwendung von quantitativen Methoden bei naturwissenschaftlichen Untersuchungen, und führte dabei das Prinzip der Stofferhaltung ein. Er stellte fest, daß bei einer chemischen Reaktion nichts verloren geht oder gewonnen wird, da das Gesamtgewicht der Produkte dem Gesamtgewicht der an der Reaktion beteiligten Stoffe gleicht. Er erkannte auch das Wesen der Elemente: daß sie Stoffe sind, die sich durch chemische Mittel nicht abbauen lassen. Er kannte nur 23 Elemente, aber er glaubte, durch weitere Untersuchungen würden sich bestimmt andere finden.

74. Lavoisier war

(A) ein berühmter Alchimist.
(B) ein Mitbegründer der Cehmie als Naturwissenschaft.
(C) der erste, der die Ideen der Chemie vertreten hat.
(D) Verfasser des Romans *Elemente der Chemie*.

75. Lavoisier glaubte, der Naturwissenschaftler sollte

(A) bei einer Untersuchung alles sorgfältig messen.
(B) die philosophische Bedeutung seiner Wissenschaft untersuchen.
(C) die Methoden der Alchimisten anwenden.
(D) Stoffe in gewissen Quantitäten untersuchen.

76. Unter "Prinzip der Stofferhaltung" versteht man:

(A) alle Stoffe, die in wissenschaftlichen Untersuchungen verwendet werden, sollten vorher sorgfältig erhalten werden.
(B) bei einer chemischen Reaktion ändert sich gar nichts.
(C) bei einer chemischen Reaktion wird das Gesamtgewicht der beteiligten Stoffe weder größer noch kleiner.
(D) mit Hilfe der Chemie kann man Stoffe länger erhalten.

77. Lavoisier kannte nur 23 Elemente, weil

(A) es nur 23 Elemente gibt.
(B) es damals nur 23 Elemente gab.
(C) er nicht daran interessiert war, neue Elemente zu finden.
(D) die Wissenschaft seiner Zeit nur 23 Elemente identifizieren konnte.

Obwohl der zweite Weltkrieg eine große Katastrophe für die ganze Welt war, ging es der amerikanischen Volkswirtschaft während des Krieges glänzend. Es gab keine Arbeitslosigkeit, und alles, was die Fabriken und Werkstätten herstellen konnten, wurde sofort gekauft. Als dann der Krieg zu Ende war, stand die amerikanische Regierung vor zwei großen Problemen: die ausländischen Märkte, auf denen vor dem Krieg amerikanische Waren verkauft worden waren, existierten nicht mehr, und Millionen von Soldaten würden bald nach Hause kommen und Arbeitsplätze verlangen. Da die Vereinigten Staaten jetzt keine Waffen mehr produzieren mußten und fast nichts im Ausland verkaufen konnten, würde es sehr schwer sein, Arbeit für alle zu finden. Wie sollte man neue Märkte schaffen und gleichzeitig die Suche nach Arbeitsplätzen so lange verschieben, bis es solche Arbeitsplätze geben würde? Die Lösung bestand aus zwei Teilen: dem Marshall-Plan, durch den die im Krieg zerstörten ausländischen Wirtschaften wiederhergestellt wurden, und dem sogenannten "G.I. Bill," durch das viele der ehemaligen Soldaten, die sonst vergeblich Arbeit hätten suchen müssen, an die Universitäten gelockt wurden.

78. Die Vereinigten Staaten konnten nach dem Krieg nur wenig exportieren, weil

(A) die Soldaten bald nach Hause kommen würden.
(B) die Länder Europas und Asiens fast nichts kaufen konnten.
(C) die amerikanischen Arbeiter nur Waffen produzieren konnten.
(D) es nicht genug Arbeiter gab.

79. Diesem Text nach war der Hauptzweck des Marshall-Plans,

(A) den Opfern des Krieges zu helfen.
(B) die Abhängigkeit Europas von Amerika zu sichern.
(C) ausländische Märkte für amerikanische Waren zu schaffen.
(D) sofort Arbeitsplätze für heimkehrende Soldaten zu schaffen.

80. Durch das "G.I. Bill" hat die amerikanische Regierung

(A) neue Arbeitsplätze für Soldaten geschaffen.
(B) den armen Europäern geholfen.
(C) neue Märkte für amerikanische Waren gefunden.
(D) viele Soldaten studieren lassen, damit sie sunächst keine Arbeitsplätze nötig hatten.

THE COLLEGE BOARD ACHIEVEMENT TEST IN GERMAN

TEST VI

ANSWER KEY

1.	A	21.	A	41.	B	61.	B
2.	B	22.	D	42.	B	62.	D
3.	A	23.	B	43.	C	63.	C
4.	B	24.	C	44.	C	64.	A
5.	C	25.	C	45.	B	65.	C
6.	B	26.	C	46.	C	66.	B
7.	C	27.	C	47.	C	67.	B
8.	C	28.	B	48.	B	68.	D
9.	D	29.	C	49.	B	69.	C
10.	A	30.	A	50.	C	70.	B
11.	A	31.	B	51.	A	71.	B
12.	B	32.	B	52.	C	72.	B
13.	C	33.	C	53.	D	73.	A
14.	C	34.	C	54.	B	74.	B
15.	D	35.	A	55.	D	75.	A
16.	C	36.	B	56.	A	76.	C
17.	B	37.	A	57.	A	77.	D
18.	A	38.	C	58.	C	78.	B
19.	D	39.	D	59.	B	79.	C
20.	A	40.	C	60.	C	80.	D

GERMAN TEST VI

DETAILED EXPLANATIONS OF ANSWERS

1. (A)

Only (A) is correct. Begegnen has the auxiliary verb sein and a dative object, and is often used with zufällig. Treffen and kennenlernen both translate the English "meet," but both require haben as auxiliary verb and an accusative object. Furthermore, treffen means "to meet by appointment," and kennenlernen means "make the acquaintance of;" neither fits here. Entgegengehen has the auxiliary verb sein and a dative object, but it means "go to meet," and would not be used with zufällig.

2. (B)

In English the number 10^9 (a one followed by nine zeros, or one thousand millions) is called a billion, but in German the same number is called eine Milliarde. Eine Billion is in German one million millions (10^{12}). Thus (B) is the correct choice. The others are wrong because only one term can be correct. This lack of agreement between English and German sometimes leads to serious translation problems. If the German Milliarde is translated into English as "billion," the reader may assume that the original text had Billion; such an assumption will of course seriously distort the understanding of the text. It is better to write out the numbers instead of trying to translate the word.

3. (A)

The German word das Wort has two plurals. Wörter is used when the words are unconnected; thus gestern, sieben, Mutter, nach, and schlafen would be five Wörter. A Wörterbuch, "dictionary," is a list of single words in alphabetical order. But if the words are connected in such a way as to make sense together, then the plural is Worte. The sentence in this question is such a group of words, so the correct choice is (A). This question is complicated somewhat by the fact that the choices are all in the dative plural (after aus), and therefore all end in –n. (B) and (C) are impossible forms; they can never occur. (D) would be correct for unrelated words.

4. (B)

To answer this question correctly you must first of all know that the word See can be either masculine or femine, and that the meaning varies with the gender. Der See means "lake," but die See means "ocean" or "sea," as in die Nordsee, the North Sea. It is assumed that you know enough geography to realize that if the city of Konstanz is in South Germany it is not on any ocean, so the correct choice will be a masculine form. This eliminates (A) and (C), since der after the prepositions an or auf can only be feminine. (C) is also wrong because auf is the wrong preposition for this usage. A ship might be auf dem See, but a town is am See. Finally, since the reference is to location rather than to motion, the dative is the correct case. Thus (D) cannot be correct, and (B) is the right answer.

5. (C)

This sentence means "This semester I have enrolled in five classes at the university." One must be very careful in choosing a German equivalent for the English "class." Die Klasse (A) refers to a group of people or things as a group; thus the members of a school class (e.g. fourth grade) would be called eine Klasse. Die Stunde (B) refers to the actual meetings of the class (Ich habe jeden Morgen um neun Uhr eine Deutschstunde). Der Kurs (C) refers to the class as course of study; this is the correct choice here, the only appropriate object for the verb belegen, which means "enroll in." "Class" can also have a socio-political meaning, as in an expression like "the middle class." The German equivalent of this is der Stand (D).

6. (B)

(B) is the correct choice. Studieren means "be a student." It refers to a status rather than to an activity as such. Thus one might say Wir haben drei Jahre studiert, but one would not use the verb studieren in reference to an activity that lasted only three hours. Thus (A), though a correct grammatical form, is the wrong word. (C) and (D) are not only the wrong word choice, but are also grammatically incorrect: (C) because studieren (like all verbs ending in -ieren) has no ge- in the past participle, and (D) because the infinitive form studieren is not correct here.

7. (C)

We are looking here for the correct German equivalent of "only." All four choices are possible equivalents, but all have different meanings, and each is correct only in its proper context. The correct choice here is (C); erst means "only" in the sense of "not until," and the sentence means "I only heard it today," i.e. "I did not hear it until today." Nur (A) has a limiting meaning; in this sentence it would mean "today is the only day on which I heard it," obviously not the correct meaning. Allein (B) and einzig (D) can mean "only," but cannot fit grammatically into the sentence given here. Ich allein habe es gehört or Ich habe es als Einziger gehört would both mean "I was the only one who heard it."

8. (C)

The correct German equivalent of "news," in the sense of "a report on the day's events, broadcast on television or radio," is die Nachrichten (C). The other words given here have different meanings. Die Neuen (A) could mean "the new people" or "the new things." Die Neuigkeiten (B) does mean "news" in the sense of "recent developments," but it does not refer to a television or radio broadcast. Das Neue (D) means "that which is new," in a sentence like Das Neue ist nicht immer das Beste.

9. (D)

This question asks for knowledge of a specific idiom. The correct choice is (D). "To think that ... is ... " expressed in German as ... (accusative object) für ... (adjective) halten. Thus (A) is wrong because it lacks the preposition für; (B) is wrong because it has the wrong preposition, the wrong case, and the wrong word order; (C) is wrong because it has a dative instead of an accusative object.

10. (A)

German expresses the idea "to cause something to be done" by the verb lassen, followed by an infinitive. Thus (A) is the correct choice here; the sentence means "We are having a new house built (for ourselves)." Though the English may imply "making" someone do something, machen is not used with this meaning; the German equivalent of "He made the students read the book" would be Er hat die Studenten gezwungen, das Buch zu lesen. So (B) is also wrong. English also frequently uses "have" ("We are having a house built"), but the German haben is never correct in this context, so (C) is also wrong. Finally, German has no equivalent of the English "We are going to build a house." The German equivalent of such a sentence would simply use the main verb (bauen) in the present or future (Wir bauen uns ein neues Haus or Wir werden uns ein neues Haus bauen).

11. (A)

The English expression "to succeed" has no exact equivalent in German; English expresses the idea personally (someone succeeds), while German expresses it impersonally, with the subject es, and the person expressed as a dative object. The verb used in German is gelingen/gelang/ist gelungen. Thus (A) is the correct choice here. (B) and (C) both try to make sie the subject, which is wrong, and (D) uses the auxiliary haben instead of the correct form of sein.

12. (B)

The modal verbs in German have some similarities with the English modal verbs, but differ in many significant ways. To answer this question correctly you must know the range of meanings of four modal verbs. (C) and (D) are fairly easy to eliminate. Magst (from mögen) indicates either "liking" or "possibility," and has no meaning that makes sense in this context. Just as speakers of English sometimes use "can" for "may" ("Can I have another cookie?"), speakers of German sometimes use forms of können when they should use forms fo dürfen; but proper usage in both languages is clearly opposed to such substitutions. To choose between (A) and (B) you must know that German müssen and English "must" are not always used in the same way. The two verbs do have approximately the same meaning in positive statements; "I must do that" and Ich muß das tun both mean "I am obliged to do that." But in negative statements the meanings are different. "I must not do that" usually means "I am obliged not to do that," while Ich muß das nicht tun means "I am not obliged to do that." Thus the English sentence expresses a negative obligation, while the German sentence indicates an absence of obligation. The idea of negative obligation is expressed in German by nicht dürfen. Thus (B) (darfst) is the correct choice here, since the sentence clearly implies a negative obligation: "You must not enter that room." If (A) (mußt) were used here, the sentence would mean "You are not obliged to enter that room."

13. (C)

In this question a choice must be made from four words, all of which are German equivalents of the English "introduce." The correct choice is (C); vorstellen is used in formally introducing one person to another. Einführen (A), when it refers to people, has no connotation of a formal presentation (Sie führte uns in diese Gruppe ein). Einleiten (B) refers to the initial part of any process, as in Der Professor leitete das Buch mit einem Vorwort ein. Einbringen (D) means "introduce a bill in a legislative body."

14. (C)

The correct choice here is weiß (C). You must first distinguish between the various words that mean "know" in German. Kennen (A) refers to some specific person, place, or thing: Ich kenne Hans Schmidt; Ich kenne Berlin; Ich kenne das Haus an der Ecke. Könne (B) means "know" only in the sense of "know how to do something;" Sie kann gut Deutsch means "She knows how to speak German well" or "She knows German well." Wissen means "know" in reference to something abstract. Further, wissen is always used if the object (the thing known) is expressed as a subordinate clause: Ich weiß, was er macht; Wir wissen, wo du wohnst; Sie weiß, daß es bald regnet. To distinguish between (C) and (D) here, you must also know that wissen, like the modal verbs, is one of the so-called "preterite-present" verbs. The present tense forms of these verbs are actually old past tense forms that have taken on present meaning. The verb wissen is cognate with the Latin videre; its fundamental meaning is "to see." Thus the present tense forms of such verbs look very much like the past tense of strong verbs. As in the past tense of strong verbs, there is no ending in the first and third person singular; ich weiß and er weiß correspond to ich kam and er kam. So wisse (D) is incorrect.

The other characteristic mark of these "preterite-present" verbs is the fact that for most of them the singular and plural have different stem vowels: weiß/wissen; kann/können; will/wollen, etc. (The only exception is sollen, which by historical accident has the same stem vowel in its singular and plural). This is because at an earlier stage of their development, most strong verbs had different vowels in the singular and plural of the past tense. This difference has been leveled today, but traces of it remain in these "preterite-present" verbs. (Another trace of the same phenomenon is the fact that the subjunctive of some verbs has a vowel different from that of the regular past tense. Normally the general subjunctive of strong verbs is formed by umlauting the past tense stem; käme is the subjunctive formed from kam. But helfen has the subjunctive hülfe, even though its past tense is half. This is because the subjunctive was derived from the past plural stem (hulfen) before it was lost).

15. (D)

All four of the possible answers are equivalents of "leave," but each of them has a different meaning. The correct choice is (D), verlassen, which means "abandon." Abfahren (A) simply means "depart;" it uses the auxiliary verb sein and cannot be used with a direct object. Liegenlassen (B) means "leave lying;" one might say Er hat das Buch auf dem Tisch liegenlassen, but one would hardly use this word in reference to people. Hinterlassen (C) usually means "leave behind at death;" one might say Er hat seinen Kindern viel Geld hinterlassen. Note that (B), (C), and (D), though they are past participles, do not have -ge-. In general, any verb whose infinitive form is not stressed on the first syllable will not have ge- in the past participle. Here the absence of stress on the first syllable is due to the presence of an unstressed prefix. In question 6 above, we noted that some verbs, notably those that are formed with ieren, are never stressed on the first syllable; they too have no initial ge- in the past participle.

16. (C)

German has several words that mean "think," but the correct choice here is glaube (C). Glauben has the basic meaning "believe," but in this context it means "to be of the opinion." Thus the sentence means "I think it will rain soon." Denken an (A) means something like "give thought to," and is usually used with some sort of subordinate clause, e.g. Ich denke daran, nach Italien zu reisen, "I am thinking of traveling to Italy." Halten (B) is used in the expression "to think that ... is ... ;" Ich halte ihn für intelligent means "I think he is intelligent." (See the discussion after question 9 above). Finally, it is important to distinguish denken "think" from danken (D), "thank."

17. (B)

The correct choice here is (B). Mann means both "husband" and "adult human male." (A) (man) is an indefinite pronoun, meaning something like "one" (Das hört man oft means "One often hears that"). Actually, man is often best translated as a passive; Man macht die Tür auf is the equivalent of "The door is opened." (C) (Mensch) means simply "human being," and would be used in a sentence like Der Mensch ist intelligenter als der Hund. (D) (Man) is wrong because of its form. Mann, the noun, is written with a capital M and double n; man, the pronoun, has only one n and is capitalized only if it is the first word of a sentence.

18. (A)

Except for gerner (B), which is an impossible form, all these words express somehow the idea of "rather." Lieber (A) is indeed the comparative form of gern, and is the correct answer here. The sentence means "My father likes to drink beer, but he would rather drink wine." Vielmehr (C) is used to indicate that the speaker has changed his/her mind: Er kommt morgen, oder vielmehr übermorgen would mean "He'll come tomorrow, or rather, I mean the day after tomorrow." Sondern (D) can be used only after a negative expression, to indicate that that expression is not correct, but something else is correct: Er ist nicht ins Kino gegangen, sondern zu Hause geblieben mean "He did not go to the movies, but rather he stayed home."

19. (D)

All four choices are equivalents of the English word "number," but again all have different meanings. The correct choice is D (Nummer); this word refers to numbers in series, such as house numbers, telephone numbers, or identification numbers. Zahl (A) usually refers to "number" as an abstract or mathematical concept, as in eine gerade Zahl, "an even number." Anzahl (B) means an indefinite number, as in eine große Anzahl von Studenten, "a large number of students." Ziffer (C) refers to the number as a written or concrete object, as in Diese Ziffer ist eine Fünf or Er konnte die römischen Ziffern nicht lesen.

20. (A)

The correct choice here is (A) (bestellt). Bestellen means "order" in the sense of "ask someone to bring or send something," and is the correct term for use in a restaurant. Befehlen (B) means "order" in the sense of "command." Ordnen (C) means "arrange, put in order." Verlangen (D) means "demand" and implies that what is demanded is one's due; it might be used to refer indirectly to a restaurant order, but it would not be used in speaking directly to the waiter. Thus all these words can be equivalents of English "order," but only (A) is correct in this sentence.

21. (A)

Only (A) is correct. The verb in a subordinate clause must be at the end, which makes (C) wrong. (B) is introduced by denn, which is not a "subordinating," but a "coordinating" conjunction, and does not affect word order. (B) would be correct if it were denn ich muß einkaufen. (D) might be correct with a different modal verb (e.g. damit ich einkaufen kann) but is not appropriate here.

22. (D)

German normally uses the present tense with the preposition seit to express an action that began in the past and continues into the present. Thus (D) is the correct answer here. (A) is wrong because it uses the perfect tense. (B) and (C) are wrong because the preposition für is used in time expressions only if the time of the time expression is **not** the same as the time implied by the verb:

Ich fahre drei Tage nach Italien.	= Driving to Italy takes me three days.
Ich fahre für drei Tage nach Italien.	= I'll drive to Italy and stay there three days.

23. (B)

The challenge here is to determine the proper order of objects in the inner field of a sentence (i.e. between the parts of the verb). This order is determined by "news value." Something that has already been mentioned has little news value, while something that has not yet been mentioned has more news value, and where there are two objects, the one with more news value comes later. A pronoun will therefore always precede a noun, since a pronoun by definition always refers to something that has already been mentioned. Thus (C) and (D) are both wrong because in them the pronoun comes after the noun. But if two nouns are used in a sentence like this, with no context, how can one tell whether or not either of them has already been mentioned? The answer is in the use of articles. If something has already been mentioned, it will have a definite article the next time it is mentioned, whereas something not yet mentioned will have an indefinite article when first mentioned. English uses the very same clues.

What did you do with that watch?	I gave **the** watch to a man.
What did you give the man?	I gave the man **a** watch.

In the first pair of sentences, "watch" occurs in the question, so it comes first, preceded by **the**, in the answer; in the second pair, "watch" is first mentioned in the answer, so it comes second, preceded by **a**. Applying this structure to German, we see that (B) is the correct choice among those given here. (A) is wrong because eine Uhr, with an indefinite article, should come second.

24. (C)

The sentence "Our teacher wants us to work diligently" is perfectly normal in English, but German does not permit the literal equivalent. If a modal verb is used in German, the subject of its complementary verb must be the same as the subject of the modal: Ich will fleißig arbeiten = "I want to work diligently." If the subjects are not the same,

German requires a subordinate clause, the literal equivalent of the rather awkward English sentence "Our teacher wants, that we work diligently." Thus the correct choice here is (C).

Both (A) and (B) are wrong because they try to use the infinitive complement, with or without zu. (D) is wrong because the verb in the subordinate clause must come at the end.

25. (C)

When a modal verb is used in a compound tense with a complementary verb, the construction is called a "double infinitive." In such cases the infinitive is substituted for the normal past participle of the modal, resulting in what looks like two infinitives together at the end of the clause. The modal always comes after the complementary verb. Thus the correct choice here is (C), the only choice with two infinitives, the latter of which is the modal. (A) tries to use the regular past participle of the modal; (B) tries to use the past participle of the complementary verb instead of the infinitive; and (D) has the modal before the complement instead of after it.

It is worth noting that nothing can come after a double infinitive in the same clause. This leads to some problems. If, for instance, a double infinitive occurs in a subordinate clause, a conflict arises, because the main verb in the subordinate clause is also supposed to come last. Here the double infinitive wins: the main verb is displaced.

> Er sagte, daß er kommen wollte.
> but
> Er sagte, daß er hat kommen wollen.

It is also worth noting that if there is no complementary verb, the normal past participle of the modal is used: Das habe ich nicht gewollt.

26. (C)

German and English both have pairs of verbs in which one of the verbs indicates an action and the only means "to cause that action." The former are always strong verbs, and the latter are weak verbs derived from the strong verbs. Thus:

Action	Cause
sitzen/saß/gesessen (sit/sat/sat)	setzen/setzte/gesetzt (set/set/set)
liegen/lag/gelegen (lie/lay/lain)	legen/legte/gelegt (lay/laid/laid)

The strong verb in such a pair is intransitive and the weak verb is transitive (i.e. it has a direct object). Furthermore, the strong verb always refers to a "continuous state" rather than to an action. If these verbs are followed by one of the prepositions that can take a dative object (referring to location) or an accusative object (referring to motion), the strong verb will always refer to location and the weak verb will always refer to motion.

The correct choice here is (C). (B) and (D) can be eliminated easily as impossible forms: liegte has the vowel of the present tense of the strong verb with a past tense weak verb ending; lagte has the past tense strong form with a weak ending. To choose between legte (A) and lag (C), note that there is no direct object and the prepositional phrase is auf dem Tisch. Both the absence of a direct object and the dative object of the preposition auf indicate that the correct verb is lag.

27. (C)

Except for archaic uses of words like "thou," English has lost its former distinction between formal and familiar address, but like most other European languages, German has kept this distinction. Today the distinction is no longer between social inferiors and superiors; instead the use of du/ihr and Sie is determined primarily by the degree of intimacy between the speaker and the one spoken to. The familiar form is used when addressing relatives, close friends, children, animals, and in prayers. The formal form is used with others. As a rule of thumb, you use du with anyone whom you address by their first name, and you use Sie with anyone whom you address with a title, such as Herr, Frau, Doktor, etc.

The Sie form is actually the third person plural form; in former times it was felt that this form was especially deferential. Ihr is of course the plural of du.

Since the person addressed in this question is called by her first name and is only one person, the correct choice is (C). (A) would be correct if you called her Frau Schmidt instead of Maria. (B) would be correct if several people were being addressed. (D), however, would never be correct, because it contains an impossible form of haben; the -b- in the stem of haben is lost in the second and third person singular forms: hast and hat.

28. (B)

In English it is quite natural to put two grammatical elements (normally the subject and an adverbial expression) before the verb in a statement:" (After dinner) (we) go to the movies." German, however, requires that the main verb in a normal statement be the second grammatical element, so only one thing can precede it. This one thing may be the subject (Ich besuche dich morgen), an object (Dich besuche ich morgen), or an adverb (Morgen besuche ich dich). So in the sentence given here, the correct choice is (B), the only choice that has one grammatical element before the verb. (A) and (C) both have two elements before the verb, and (D) has the verb first.

Actually, it is quite possible to begin a German sentence with a verb, but such sentences are not simple statements. An "exhortation," sometimes called a "first person imperative," begins with a verb, but the subject always follows immediately. Thus it would be possible to rearrange (D) to read Gehen wir nach dem Essen ins Kino, meaning "Let's go to the movies after dinner." But (D) as it stands here cannot begin a grammatically correct sentence.

29. (C)

There are two kinds of conditional sentences: those that have not been, or will not be, fulfilled, and those that may or may not be, or have been, fulfilled. The former are called "closed" conditions or "contrary to fact" conditions and use the subjunctive; the latter are called "open" conditions and use the indicative.

Contrary to fact:
Present:
Wenn sie hier wäre, würde ich sie sehen.
If she were here, I would see her. (Since I don't see her, she is not here.)

Past:
Wenn sie hier gewesen wäre, hätte ich sie gesehen.
If she had been here, I would have seen her. (Since I did not see her, she was not here.)

Open:
Present:
Wenn ich Geld habe, mache ich Urlaub.
If I have money I take a vacation. (I may or may not have money.)

Past:
Wenn ich Geld hatte, machte ich Urlaub. (Sometimes I did not have money, so I had no vacation.)

In this question the use of the indicative form in the second part of the sentence indicates that it is an open condition, one that may or may not be fulfilled; "If it rains tomorrow we will not work (but if it does not rain we will work)." So the indicative is called for in the first part as well. Thus the correct choice is (C), the only indicative form. (A) and (B) are subjunctive forms that would be correct if there were also a subjunctive form in the second part of the sentence. (D) is also a subjunctive form, but is a past subjunctive, so it is wrong because the verb in the second part of the sentence is present indicative.

30. (A)
This illustrates the other kind of conditional sentence, the "contrary to fact" condition, in the past. The sentence means: "If I had earned more money I would have been able to take a vacation." The correct choice is (A), the only past subjunctive form. (B) is a perfect indicative; (C) is a present indicative; and (D) is a variant form of the present subjunctive.

For the use of the double infinitive hätte --- machen können see the explanation of question 25 above.

31. (B)

Although contemporary colloquial German does use indicative verbs in some indirect statements, the need for the subjunctive is emphasized in this sentence by the statement of disbelief; the subjunctive is commonly used to indicate that the speaker doubts what is being indirectly reported. Thus choices (A) and (C) here can be eliminated at once because they are indicative forms. Wäre (D) is a subjunctive, but it is not the right word; it makes no sense in this sentence. That leaves (B) as the only possible correct choice.

There are two subjunctive conjugations in German, one based on the present stem of the verb and one based on the past stem. The latter, called variously the "general subjunctive" or "subjunctive II," is used anywhere a subjunctive is called for. The former, called the "special subjunctive," the "indirect discourse subjunctive," or "subjunctive I," is used today primarily in indirect quotations. Even in indirect quotations, its use is usually limited to the third person singular, since its other forms look and sound too much like indicative forms. The third person singular, where the indicative ends in –t and the subjunctive ends in –e, is clearly distinct. The form habe, appearing here as choice (C), is the third person singular form of the "indirect discourse subjunctive."

32. (B)

Während is one of the prepositions that take a genitive object; the only correct choice here is (B). (A) is wrong because the nominative form (der Tag) can never be used as the object of a preposition. (C) and (D) have dative and accusative objects respectively; other prepositions use these cases, but während does not. Other common prepositions that have genitive objects are wegen, trotz, and (an) statt.

33. (C)

Warten is usually followed by a prepositional phrase consisting of auf and an accusative object (Ich warte auf dich), or by a dependent clause. If a dependent clause is used, it differs significantly from the corresponding English idiom. In English we say "I am waiting for you to come," using an infinitive construction, but German does not allow this. Hence (A) and (B) are both wrong here. "To wait for something or someone" is expressed in German with warten auf---, but German does not permit a dependent clause to be the immediate object of a preposition, so we may not say Ich warte auf daß du kommst. Instead, the dependent clause is anticipated by a da- preceding the preposition, and we say Ich warte darauf, daß du kommst, as in (C), the correct choice. The literal equivalent in English would be "I am waiting for this, that you come," and the clause daß due kommst really functions as an "expansion" or "explanation" of darauf.

34. (C)

The German equivalent of "without - - - -ing" usually requires ohne and an infinitive with zu. Thus the correct choice here is (C). (A) is a literal translation, unintelligible to a German, of the English idiom "without visiting me." (B) lacks the necessary zu. Another way to express this idiom in German is with ohne daß; the addition of daß would make (D) acceptable (ohne daß sie mich besucht hat), but without the daß it is wrong.

35. (A)

The idea of "purpose" can be expressed in German in several ways. If the subject of both clauses is the same, as in the first part of this sentence ("I" am both the one who works and the one who studies), then the normal way is with um and an infinitive with zu. However, if the subjects are not the same, the idea is expressed with damit and a finite verb. Thus the correct choice here is (A), and the second part of the sentence means "but my father worked so that his children could study." (B) is wrong because the um----zu construction cannot be used if the subjects are different. (C) is wrong because um cannot be combined with a finite verb in this context. (D) is wrong because damit requires a finite verb, not an infinitive.

36. (B)

Since es gibt always has an accusative object, only an accusative form can be the correct choice here. The word Student has the ending -en in all forms except the nominative singular. Thus (C), which can only be nominative, is wrong. Since Student is masculine, the accusative form of the preceding kein must be either keinen (singular) or keine (plural). Thus (D) must also be wrong. (A) and (B) are both acceptable accusative forms, but (A) is singular and (B) is plural. To choose between them you must realize that the relative pronoun in the next clause is plural. Since the relative clause depends on its antecedent for number and gender, a plural relative pronoun means that the antecedent must also be plural. Thus (B), the plural form, is the correct choice.

37. (A)

Most intransitive verbs that indicate motion or change require sein as their auxiliary verb in the perfect, and kommen is no exception, so (C) and (D) can be eliminated at once. To choose between (A) and (B), however, you must be careful to use the German rather than the English idiom. In English, a word like "police" is usually thought of as plural. We say "The police are coming" rather than "The police is coming." But in German die Polizei is singular, and the verb used with it must therefore also be singular. Thus the correct choice here is (A).

38. (C)

(A) is the literal translation of the English idiom "are interested in," and is impossible in German. The other three choices are the same except for the preposition used; the only correct choice is (C). It is worth noting that there is a related idiom that uses an; we can say Ich bin an der klassischen Musik interessiert.

39. (D)

This sentence means "Have you heard the new tenor sing?" The verbs helfen, hören, sehen, and lassen function like modal verbs, in that they make use of the "double infinitive" construction when used in compound tenses with another verb. Thus the correct choice here is (D). (A) has two infinitives, but they are in the wrong order. Just as the modal verb must be the second infinitive (see the explanation of question 35 above), so these verbs must also come after the complementary verb. (B) and (C) are not double infinitives. To illustrate further the use of these verbs:

Wir haben den Arzt kommen lassen.	We sent for the doctor.
Ich habe ihnen arbeiten helfen.	I helped them work.
Sie hat uns kommen sehen.	She saw us coming.

40. (C)

To express the idea that one thing varies as a function of something else, German uses je - - desto (or je - - um so). they must be used in a definite order: the "independent" variable is preceded by je, and the "dependent" variable is preceded by desto. Thus the sentence given here means "The older I get, the more slowly I work." The placement of je and desto has to indicate that working more slowly is a function of aging. Thus the correct choice here is (C). (A) is an attempt to bring over from English the idiom "the more - - the more." (B) is meaningless. (D) uses the right words, but in the wrong order.

41. (B)

Only (B) is correct. Als, wenn, and wann all translate the English "when," but with different meanings. Wann is used only in questions, direct or indirect (Wann kommt der Zug an? or Weißt du, wann der Zug ankommt?). Als is used to refer to a single action in the past, no matter how long that action may have lasted (Als ich ankam, hatten sie schon gegessen or Als ich jung war, wohnte ich in Berlin). Wenn is used for all present and future actions, and (as here) for repeated action in the past. Repeated action is indicated here by immer. Während means "while," but is not appropriate here because the action described is repeated.

42. (B)

Es gibt must be followed by an accusative, and Wein is masculine, so the correct answer is (B), the only word that can be masculine accusative. (A) (kein) could be masculine nominative or neuter nominative/accusative. (C) (nicht) is wrong because nicht is not used to negate a noun; it negates verbs: Er kommt nicht. (D) (keiner) cannot possibly be accusative, but it could be the nominative masculine singular if the word were used as a pronoun, i.e. not as a modifier: Keiner von meinen Brüdern studiert in Heidelberg.

43. (C)

When a question or statement is phrased negatively, doch is used in the response to indicate that the contrary is true. In this case the question ("Is there no more wine?") is expressed negatively, and the answer is clearly that there is wine, and that it is on the table. Thus (C) is the correct choice. (A) (Ja) is never used to respond to a negative question. (B) (Nein) means that the answer is also negative: there is no more wine. Since the only possible responses to such a negatively phrased question are nein and doch, (D) (Nicht) is also wrong.

44. (C)

Both an and auf are prepositions that can have dative or accusative objects, depending on whether the verb with which they are used indicates motion (accusative) or location (dative). This verb indicates location, so the preposition, whichever one is used, will have a dative object. Some speakers of English might be tempted to choose the preposition an because it sounds like English "on," but this is deceptive; auf corresponds to English "on," while an corresponds to English "at." The correct preposition here is auf, and since Tisch is masculine, the correct answer is (C). (A) and (B) are wrong because an is the wrong preposition, and (D) is wrong because den is either accusative singular or dative plural, neither of which is correct here.

45. (B)

The possessives normally modify nouns: mein Haus, mein Freund, meine Mutter. In this usage, the masculine and neuter forms of the nominative singular and the neuter accusative singular have no endings. But when one of these forms is used as a pronoun instead of modifying a noun, endings are required, and they are the endings normally associated with these cases: meiner in the nominative masculine singular and mein(e)s in the nominative and accusative neuter singular. so the correct choice in question 45 is (B); the word has to refer to Wagen (masculine) and be the subject of its clause, and (B) is the only form given that can be nominative masculine. (A) (mein), having no ending, can only be a modifier; (C) (meins) is neuter; and (D) (meinen) is accusative.

46. (C)

This sentence requires a passive verb in the past tense, and only (C) is correct. The passive in German is constructed with forms of werden and the past participle of the verb used. (B) and (C) both offer forms of werden, but the context demans a past tense, and (B) is present. In English the passive is made with forms of the verb "to be" ("The door is opened every day at nine." "The criminal was seen in Chicago.") Hence speakers of English sometimes try to make the passive in German using forms of sein. (A) is wrong because the verb war is the too-literal translation of English "was." (D) (hat) is wrong because it cannot be passive. A sentence like Er hat mir den Wagen geschenkt is grammatically correct, but it is not passive, and the sentence to be completed here requires a passive.

47. (C)

English uses the word "where" in several different ways, while German has a different word for each of these usages. Wo refers only to location: "Where is he?"; wohin refers to motion toward a destination: "Where is he going?"; woher refers to motion away from some other place: "Where is he coming from?" Since the verb here, wohnen, refers to location, the correct choice is (C). Some speakers of English are confused by the fact that the German word wer (D) looks and sounds similar to the English "where." This is unfortunate, since wer means "who."

48. (B)

German has two possible ways to express English "if": the conditional "if" ("If it rains we can't go.") is expressed by wenn, but the "if" that is the equivalent of "whether" is expressed by ob. This sentence is of the latter sort, so (A) is wrong and (B) is the correct choice. Weder (C) and Wetter (D) both sound something like "whether," but have entirely different meanings; weder means "neither" and Wetter means "weather."

49. (B) 50. (C)

Both these questions are concerned with the proper endings for adjectives used after definite articles and other der- words (e.g. dieser, jeder, jener), the so-called "weak" endings. The ending -e is used in five cases: the nominative singular in all three genders, and the accusative singular feminine and neuter. The ending -en is used in all other cases. In question 49, der Mann is masculine nominative, and the correct ending on a following adjective is -e, so the correct choice is (B). (A) (alter) is the nominative masculine singular "strong" ending, to be used when there is no preceding determiner or when the preceding determiner is ein. (B) (alten) has the wrong ending, and (D) (älter) can only be the comparative form; the -er is not an ending here at all, but a suffix indicating "comparative."

In question 50, the form der can only be the feminine dative singular, since the verb helfen requires a dative object and Frau is feminine. The correct adjective ending is therefore -en, and the correct choice is (C). (A) (junger) would be correct if there were no preceding article, since it has the dative feminine "strong" ending -er. (D) (jünger) is like älter in question 49, a comparative form with no ending.

51. (A)

This question shows a fundamental difference between English and German grammar: it is possible in German to have a sentence with no subject. The correct choice is (A) (Dem Studenten), a dative expression. When an active sentence is transformed into the corresponding passive sentence, the normal transformation process is as follows: the accusative object (if any) of the active sentence becomes the subject of the passive sentence, and the subject of the active sentence becomes the agent in the passive sentence. This is true for both English and German. Thus:

I see him.	Ich sehe ihn.
He is seen by me.	Er wird von mir gesehen.

But if the verb in the active sentence requires a dative object in German, there is no accusative object, and hence there is nothing that can become the subject of the passive sentence. The dative object remains dative, and the passive sentence simply has no subject. In English we no longer make any distinction between dative and accusative; any object in the active sentence can become the subject of the passive sentence. So when a German verb has a dative object, the sentence structure is quite different from English.

I help him.	Ich helfe ihm.
He is helped by me.	Ihm wird von mir geholfen.

The sentence in question 51 is a bit more complex, but its basic structure is: Dem Studenten wurde von den Eltern gedankt, which corresponds to Ihm wird von mir geholfen.

Many speakers of English would choose (C), because Der Student is the nominative form, which is what English would use. (B) is wrong because Student must have the ending -en in all forms except the nominative singular. And (D) is wrong because it is either accusative (the wrong case) or dative plural; the dative form might be correct, but if it were, the relative pronoun and the verb in the following relative clause would have to be plural as well.

52. (C)

A relative pronoun can refer back to a specific word as antecendent, or it can refer to the whole preceding clause. If it refers to a specific word, it must have the same gender and number as that word, but its case is determined by its use in its own clause. If it refers to the whole preceding clause and functions as subject or direct object in its own clause, it takes the form was. In this sentence the relative pronoun must be nominative, since it functions as the subject in its own clause. The only plausible specific antecedent is eine Blume, which is feminine, but there is no feminine nominative among the choices. So (C) (was) is the only correct choice. (A) and (B) could both be relative pronouns, but they are wrong because they are not nominative feminine singular. Because English uses "that" as an all-purpose relative pronoun ("the man that I met" "the ball that hit me"), some English speakers assume that daß functions the same way in German; unfortunately, this is not true, so (D) is also wrong.

53. (D)

Street addresses are almost always given with the article preceding the name of the street, so (A) and (C) are wrong because they lack an article. There remains the question of which preposition to choose; German usually prefers in, so (D) is the correct choice.

54. (B)

If (A) (no preposition) were correct, die Frage would be the direct object of antworten. Since antworten cannot have a direct object, (A) must be wrong. As in question 53, there remains the problem of which preposition to choose. The correct choice is (B) (auf); the others are simply wrong.

55. (D)

In referring to parts of the body and articles of clothing, German prefers a "dative of reference" instead of a possessive. Thus such references often have two objects, one in the accusative, indicating the actual body part of article of clothing, and one in the dative indicating the person to whom the body part or piece of clothing belongs. In question 55, (A) is grammatically correct, but is idiomatically doubtful. (B) is wrong because both objects are accusative. (C) is wrong because both objects are dative. Thus (D), with a dative object of the person and accusative object of the thing, is the correct choice. Other sentences of this type are:

Er gab es mir in die Hand.	He put it into my hand.
Sie kämmte dem Kind die Haare.	She combed the child's hair.
Ich muß mir die Schuhe anziehen.	I have to put on my shoes.

Note, however, that if the person is the only object, it will often be in the accusative:

Ich muß mich anziehen.	I have to get dressed.
Ich habe mich gewaschen.	I washed (myself).

56. (A) 57. (A)

Two things are being tested here: the placement of adverbs in the inner field of a sentence, and the proper way to express dates. In general, when there are several adverbial expressions in a sentence (i.e. expressions that answer questions like where? when? how?), they occur in a certain order. Time-expressions usually come first, and place-expressions usally come last. Other kinds of expressions, such as "means" or "accompaniment" come after time-expressions and before place-expressions. In this sentence, therefore, the date must precede the place; in Bonn must be the second of the two adverbial expressions, so (C) and (D) are both wrong.

In German there are two legitimate ways to express a date: either with no preposition at all, as in (A) and (D), or with the expression im Jahre, as in (C). But since (C) has the adverbial expressions in the wrong order, (A) must be the correct choice. Note that German does not use the preposition in to express dates.

58. (C)

German uses the genitive case to express indefinite time, so the correct choice here is (C). Expressions of definite time are in the accusative, as in (A), or in a sentence like Ich habe ihn letzten Dienstag gesehen, but here the indefinite article is used, and therefore there is no indication here of definite time. Neither the dative alone (B) nor the nominative alone (D) is ever used in time expressions.

59. (B)

Aber (A) is a co-ordinating conjunction; it stands between two clauses and belongs to neither, so used alone it has no effect on the word order of a following clause. If aber were the correct word here, there would be something in front of the verb haben to keep it from being the first element in the clause; since there is no such thing here, (A) must be wrong. Obwohl (C) is a subordinating conjunction; any clause it introduces will have its finite verb at the end. Since the finite verb here (haben) is not at the end, (C) must be wrong. If there are two few words before the verb in (A), there are too many in (D). The verb must be the second grammatical element in the clause, but (D) has two separate adverbs (trotzdem and gestern) before the verb. So (D) is also wrong. That leaves (B) as the only possible correct choice. In (B), aber has no effect on word order, and trotzdem "nevertheless" is the single grammatical element before the verb.

60. (C)

Some verbs in German must have an accusative object. In English we can say "She turned around and looked at me," but in German the subject of a verb like drehen, bewegen, or entwickeln must act upon some object or upon itself. Thus if there is no other object, such a verb will have reflexive object.

Sie drehte den Stuhl um.	She turned the chair around.
Sie drehte sich um.	She turned (herself) around.

Thus (A) is wrong because there must be some object after this verb. (D) is wrong because langsam is an adverb, not an object. (B) is wrong because ihr cannot be an accusative object. (C) is the correct choice.

Note that although the reflexive pronouns for the first and second persons are identical with the personal pronouns, the third person has only one "all-purpose" reflexive pronoun, sich. It is singular and plural, dative and accusative, masculine, feminine and neuter.

61. (B)

This text deals with the political and economic development of cities in late medieval Europe. As the cities became more powerful economically, they demanded more political independence, and got it by escaping the authority of local nobles.

For question 61, (B) is the only correct answer that can be obtained from the text. The main point of the first sentence is that there were some large cities, so (A) is wrong. Among the cities listed are three in the north; hence (C) cannot be correct. No cities with more than 50,000 people are mentioned, and the text implies that Cologne, with almost 30,000 was the largest city in Germany, so (D) is not correct.

62. (D)

(D) (that the cities were becoming more and more powerful economically) is the only correct answer to question 62. (A) says that the cities were economically weak; (B) says that they had no interest in politics; and (C) states that they wanted to be dependent of the nobility. The text, however, states that the growing economic power of the cities was associated with a desire for political power, and that made the people in the cities want to be free of the rule of the nobility.

63. (C)

To answer question 63 you must understand that the text defines a "free city" as one that is subject only to the king. Thus (C) is correct. Some cities were members of the Hanseatic League (A), but that was not what made them "free cities." Free cities were those that had escaped the rule of the lesser nobility (B) ("counts and dukes") and were subject directly to the king. (D) is wrong for several reasons, but mainly because the German word "frei" is not the equivalent of English "free" in the sense of "without cost."

64. (A)

(A) is the only correct answer to question 64. The text states that before World War II most German children spoke dialect at home and learned Hochdeutsch in school. So (B) (that they only spoke dialect in school) and (C) (that they learned dialect in school) are both clearly wrong. The text further makes it clear that they did speak dialect with their parents: it says that they spoke it at home, and it says that some thought the dialect was a secret language which they shared with their parents, so (D) (that they did not speak dialect with their parents) is also wrong.

65. (C)

Question 65 asks why many married couples in the time after World War II did not speak dialect at home. The reason given is that many people in that period married people who came from different regions and hence spoke different dialects. Thus only (C) is correct; most Germans could speak a dialect, but many couples had no common dialect. (A) is wrong because each could speak a dialect, even though they had no dialect in common. (B) states that they wanted to have a secret language; the text uses this term, but in reference to a different pair of generations. (D) is wrong because the text nowhere says that they wanted to forget their home regions.

66. (B)

The whole text leads up to the final sentence and explains why many Germans today do not speak any dialect. The only answer to question 66 that can be justified from the text is (B) (because their parents did not speak dialect at home). (A) (because their parents died early) and (D) (because they moved often as children) are possible reasons why Germans might not speak dialect today, but neither is mentioned in the text. (C) (because they learned High German in school) is irrelevant; dialects were normally learned at home.

67. (B)

This text is concerned with main character in the novel *The Tin Drum*, by Günter Grass. Oskar Matzerath is a most unusual child: from the moment of his birth he is totally aware of what is happening around him, and on his third birthday he stops growing by an an act of his own will. He also has two most unusual talents: he can not only shatter glass with his voice, but can cut glass in specific forms as well, and he can influence people's thoughts and moods with his drumming. Grass uses Oskar to show Germans their weaknesses and problems.

The correct answer to question 67 is (B): the text makes it clear that Oskar is a very unusual child, so (A) (that he is normal) is obviously wrong. (C) is wrong because Oskar is not the author, but the main character in the novel. And (D) (that he is an unusually large child) is wrong because the text implies that he grew normally until his third birthday, then stopped growing entirely, so he would be an unusually small child from the age of three on.

68. (D)

(D) is the correct answer to question 68: the text states that because he looks like a three-year-old, Oskar is often not punished for doing things for which a bigger child or an adult would be punished. (A) is wrong because it says that he is always caught and punished when he does something bad, and (C) is wrong because the text does not say that he is not seen because of his size. (B) (that he is accompanied by a bigger child) is simply irrelevant.

69. (C)

The answer to question 69 is (C): Oscar can influence the thoughts and moods of people (seduce them) by means of his drumming. (A) is wrong because it implies that he needs tools to break glass, whereas the text states that he does it with his voice. (B) is wrong for the same reason; he breaks glass with his voice, not by drumming. And (D) is wrong because the text does not say that his voice disturbs people, only that it breaks or cuts glass.

70. (B)

For question 70 only (B) is correct: the text states clearly that Grass intends this novel to show the Germans their weaknesses and problems. Thus (A), that the Germans have no weaknesses or problems, is clearly false. (C) is wrong because the text does not say that Germans should imitate Oskar, and (D) is wrong because neither Grass nor this text says that all Germans should remain children.

71. (B)

A policeman stops a motorist who is driving too fast for safety. When he asks why the man is driving so fast, he gets an outrageous answer: it is almost dark, and the motorist does not want to drive after dark because his headlights are broken; furthermore, he does not want to drive without headlights because his brakes do not function.

Question 71 asks why the policeman stops the motorist. The only correct answer is (B) (it is dangerous to drive so fast in the city). The text does not imply that the driver is drunk (A), and the policeman does not suspect that the driver is rushing because it is getting dark (D). (C) is a conventional question, asked of anyone in a hurry, but seldom taken seriously: "Where's the fire?"

72. (B)

Question 72 requires that you draw an inference. The text does not state explicitly why the driver is impatient, but it is nevertheless clear that it is because he knows, as the policeman does not, why he is driving so fast and how important it is that he get home before dark. Thus the correct answer is (B). (A) is wrong because the policeman does not scold the driver. (C) is wrong because, as the policeman's question brings out, they are not heading for the hospital. And (D) is wrong because the man seems not at all reluctant to explain why he is driving so fast; he only wants to do it quickly so he can continue on his way.

73. (A)

Question 73 gets to the point of the story. To the reader's astonishment, the driver seems to think that his reasons for driving so fast are perfectly valid, and he expects to be allowed to continue. Thus (A) is the correct answer. It is not really surprising that the policeman does not scold the driver; the policeman does not yet know what the driver is thinking. So (B) is wrong. (C) (that the driver is driving so fast), and (D) (that the passenger has nothing to say), are not surprising.

74. (B)

This text is concerned with the origins of the science of chemistry. Chemistry began as alchemy, but sometime before the 18th century new ideas were proposed, which led to the release of chemistry from bondage to alchemy. The process was completed with the publication in 1789 of Lavoisier's book *Elements of Chemistry*. He emphasized the importance of quantitative methods and introduced several important ideas, among them a) the conservation of matter (in any chemical reaction no matter is lost or gained, since careful measurement reveals that the total weight of the products of that reaction is equal to the total weight of the original matter), and b) the nature of a chemical element, a substance that cannot be further broken down by chemical means.

The text makes it clear that although Lavoisier played an important role in the foundation of the science of chemistry, the beginnings of that science antedated his work. Thus in question 74, (B) (that he was a co-founder of chemistry) is correct, and (C) (that he was the first to propose the ideas of modern chemistry) is wrong. (A) is wrong because Lavoisier was not an alchemist, and (D) is wrong because, though Lavoisier was indeed the author of *Elements of Chemistry*, it is not a novel.

75. (A)

Using quantitative methods means, among other things, paying close attention to measurements in all scientific experiments. so the correct answer to question 75 is (A). The text states that the alchemists saw natural science as part of philosophy, and that Lavoisier rejected that idea. Thus (B) (that the scientist should be searching for the philosophical meaning of science) and (C) (that the scientist should use the methods of the alchemist) are both wrong. Finally, (D) is wrong because the text says nothing about the quantities of matter to be investigated.

76. (C)

To answer question 76 you must simply recognize the correct definition of ther term "Principle of Conservation of Matter." It means that in a chemical reaction no matter is gained or lost; careful measurement shows that the total weight of the matter involved is the same before and after the reaction. (Of course this was proposed in the 18th century; we know now that some matter is indeed lost by being converted into energy, but people in those days had neither Einstein's equations nor very precise measuring devices). So the correct answer to question 76 is (C). (A) says that all matter to be used in scientific experiments should be carefully stored (conserved) beforehand; (B) says that in a chemical reaction nothing at all changes, which is obviously not true; and (D) says that materials can be kept for a longer time by means of chemical preservatives.

77. (D)

Question 77 asks how it was that Lavoisier knew only 23 chemical elements. The answer, both from history and from the text, is that the people of his time had managed to identify only that many elements. So (D) is correct. (A) says that only 23 elements exist, which is of course wrong, and (B) implies that the nature of the universe has changed since then: there are more elements now than there were then. (C) says that Lavoisier was not interested in finding more elements, but the text implies that he was quite interested in this question, and expected that more elements would be identified in time.

78. (B)

This text provides economic justification for two measures taken by the American Government after W W II: the Marshall Plan and the G.I. Bill. During the war there was no unemployment (most of the workers were in the armed services) and the war produced a market for everything the country could produce. After the war, however, the domestic market was much smaller, and the old foreign markets no longer existed, since much of Europe and Asia had been reduced to rubble. Furthermore, the returning soldiers would be seeking work, and there would not be enough work for all of them until foreign markets could be restored. So the government tried a two-pronged solution to the problem: the Marshall Plan was intended to enable foreign countries to rebuild their economies, and the G.I. Bill sent the veterans back to school, thus keeping them out of the job market for a while.

Question 78 asks why the U.S. could not export very much after the war. The correct answer is (B) (that the countries of Europe and Asia were not able to buy). (A) (that the soldiers were coming home) is irrelevant; (C) (that American workers could only produce munitions) is not true; and (D) (that there were not enough workers) is precisely the opposite of the truth; there would soon be too many workers.

79. (C)

Although the Marshall Plan did have several purposes, only one of which was the rebuilding of foreign markets, question 79 specifically asks you to answer with reference to this text, which states that the main purpose of the Marshall Plan was to rebuild foreign markets. Thus the correct answer is (C). (A) (to help the victims of the war) is actually true. It was one of the purposes of the Marshall Plan, but it is not the correct answer to this question, because it is not the main pupose as given in this text. (B) (to emphasize Europe's dependence on America) is too cynical to be correct, and (D) (to provide immediate jobs for returning soldiers) is simply wrong.

80. (D)

Question 80 asks what the G.I. Bill accomplished. It did not create new jobs at once (A); it did not help the poor Europeans (B); and it did not find new markets for American goods (C). But it did enable many soliders to go to college, thus keeping them out of the job market temporarily (D), so (D) is the correct answer.